GQ
HOW TO WIN AT LIFE

A Firefly Book

Published by Firefly Books Ltd. 2018

First printing

Publisher Cataloging-in-Publication Data (U.S.)

Library of Congress Control Number: 2018939121

Library and Archives Canada Cataloguing in Publication

Burton, Charlie, author
   GQ : how to win at life : the expert guide to excelling at everything
you do / Charlie Burton.
Includes index.
ISBN 978-0-228-10087-4 (hardcover)
   1. Men--Life skills guides. I. Title. II. Title: How to win at life : the
expert guide to excelling at everything you do. III. Title: Expert guide to
excelling at everything you do.
HQ1090.B86 2018   646.70081   C2018-901899-2

Published in the United States by
Firefly Books (U.S.) Inc.
P.O. Box 1338, Ellicott Station
Buffalo, New York 14205

Published in Canada by
Firefly Books Ltd.
50 Staples Avenue, Unit 1
Richmond Hill, Ontario L4B 0A7

Printed and bound in China

First published
by Mitchell Beazley,
a division of Octopus Publishing Group Ltd
Carmelite House
50 Victoria Embankment
London EC4Y 0DZ

Commissioning Editor Joe Cottington
Managing Editor Sybella Stephens
Copy Editor Helen Ridge
Creative Director Jonathan Christie
Illustrator Dave Hopkins
Designer Jeremy Tilston
Production Controller Dasha Miller

FOR EMILY

GQ
HOW TO WIN AT LIFE

THE EXPERT GUIDE TO EXCELLING AT EVERYTHING YOU DO

CHARLIE BURTON

FIREFLY BOOKS

CONTENTS

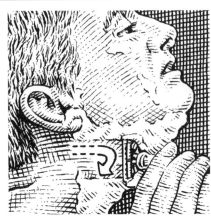

INTRODUCTION

INTRO-
DUCTION

>> In 1859, the Scottish author Samuel Smiles published a book that spawned a genre. It offered its readers advice on everything from confidence building to money management, all illustrated by inspiring tales from great lives. Want to improve your business? Learn from the way Napoleon organized his military operations. Struggling with a setback? Consider how Sir Walter Scott used his time recovering from an injury to embark on writing a great poem. Entitled *Self-Help*, Smiles's work was to become a runaway success; by the time he died, in 1904, it had sold more than 250,000 copies.

The genre has since evolved in ways that probably would have left Smiles aghast. The demeanor of self-improvement books tends to reflect that of the time in which they are produced. In recent years, one trend has exploded on the personal development bookshelf that seems to have especially captured the zeitgeist: the "believe it and it will come true" phenomenon. Looking inward rather than outward, it champions emotions over authorities. Is it a coincidence that it has blossomed in the same era in which the British politician Michael Gove felt confident claiming that people had "had enough of experts"?

This book has not had enough of experts. Its origins stretch back to a *GQ* column called "Bring Your 'A' Game." The idea was to take something that a man might reasonably want to do, and present a five-step guide to doing it really well. It would have been hubris to think we had all the answers, so we often found ourselves consulting specialists. Soon we realized we were amassing more insider knowledge than we could fit on the page. The consequence is the book you're holding in your hands; inside, you will find more detailed versions of those magazine pieces alongside a whole host of brand-new entries. This collection is not meant to offer a grand system or philosophy. Think of it instead as a volume more in the mode of Smiles's: an instant set of mentors to whom you can turn when you want to step up your game in everything from work to sport, travel to romance, food to fashion and much more.

In certain areas, *GQ* will be your mentor. Since 1988, the magazine has been the leading monthly chronicle of men's fashion and lifestyle. So when it comes to tying a scarf, defining your signature look, getting to grips with a bow tie — or something else that falls in our wheelhouse — you're going to hear from us directly.

For most of this book, however, you'll be referred to a league of external experts, 63 in all. Naturally, some of them will be familiar names. I visited Jamie Oliver for a guide to cooking the perfect steak, for instance, and interviewed Tracey Emin about how to hang a picture like an artist. To find out how to dive gracefully into a pool, I went to Tom Daley; to learn how to start a successful business, I phoned Sir Richard Branson and he dispensed advice from a hammock on Necker Island (now there is someone who is really winning at life). On these pages you'll also encounter wisdom from the likes of William Hague, Dynamo, Alastair Campbell, Andy McNab and Jorja Smith.

Alongside the celebrities, I consulted people with whom you may not yet be acquainted but who are the undisputed authorities in their fields. People such as Jon Kabat-Zinn. In 1979, Kabat-Zinn set up the Stress Reduction Clinic at the University of Massachusetts Medical School. Its purpose was to use meditation to help chronically ill patients who were not responding well to conventional treatment. At a time when the practice was associated with flaky,

New Age mysticism, Kabat-Zinn, with his Ph.D in molecular biology, took a scientific approach to meditation. Slowly, what he dubbed "Mindfulness-Based Stress Reduction" went mainstream. If you've ever wondered where the current mindfulness boom came from — well, he's its founding father. Who better to ask for pointers on how to meditate?

It was also fascinating to speak to Joe Navarro. When he was a special agent at the FBI, he caught spies by analyzing body language. His most famous case began during a routine interview with a US soldier who had become a person of interest. Every time he mentioned the name of a recently arrested traitor, the soldier's cigarette would tremor in his hand. "Everybody kept saying: 'That's nonsense, you can't base an investigation on a shaking cigarette,'"

Navarro told me. "Eventually I got him to admit that there was a larger conspiracy — and that the nuclear 'go' codes had been compromised." Navarro subsequently became a consultant on nonverbal communication, and in the chapter Work & Career you'll find his guide to the psychology behind a successful handshake.

Putting this book together was an education. Along the way, I learned why sugar can help you make a brilliant speech, the one word to use if you want to win an argument, and how a chair can save your life. A memorable tip came courtesy of Oli Barrett, "the most connected man in Britain," according to *Wired* magazine. During our interview about networking, he referenced a contact who had recently sold a company for more than a billion dollars. "The secret of their success," he said, "was sending handwritten notes to investors they met along the way." You only have to look at my out-tray to see how I've taken that to heart.

Occasionally, I came to rethink my entire approach to something altogether. Take cooking a rib-eye steak. I thought I had that largely figured out — a steak's a steak, right? When I met Jamie Oliver in his test kitchen, however, it was fast apparent that I was going to learn a considerably more sophisticated technique than my own. "With a steak, you are in the realm of the most expensive, longest-living beast in the common food chain," he explained. "Therefore, to treat it like chicken means you're a mug, to treat it like a pig means you're a mug." His favored method is packed with clever twists; it has swiftly become my favored method, too.

Since childhood, I have always enjoyed teaching myself skills from books. The sense that something extraordinary is achievable, if you simply follow the steps, has led me to pore over volumes on guitar playing, kung fu, card magic, poker, bartending, even (and I'm not proud of this) harmonica playing. Sometimes I learned things that I really had no use for at all. On my bookshelf you'll find a tome on stage hypnotism, for instance, and another on lock picking. But there's something intriguing about understanding how people do things, even if you never plan on doing them yourself. Hence the final chapter of this book, which is about dealing with the unexpected. I hope that neither you nor I will ever need to survive a kidnapping, save ourselves from choking or land a plane with engine failure.

But if you do, good luck.

1:

FOOD & DRINK

"Cooking is an art," the food science maven Nathan Myhrvold once observed. "But all art requires knowing something about the techniques." That's where this chapter comes in. The closest you're going to find to a recipe here is our guide to cooking the perfect steak — a technical feat more than anything else. The rest are all hands-on skills; some of them are tune-ups (improve your knife skills, deal with a broken wine cork), but some of them will ask you to re-learn something entirely. Thought you knew how to barbecue? Think again...

COOK THE PERFECT STEAK

>> Steak deserves to be treated with respect. Rearing beef uses significantly more resources than poultry or pork, so buy it for a special occasion and make sure you get the good stuff. "Dry aging for 20–40 days on the bone is essential," says Jamie Oliver. The celebrity chef-cum-restaurateur advises buying from a butcher rather than a supermarket, and considers grass-fed rib-eye to be the ultimate cut. Buy a 4-cm- (1½-in-) thick portion to share. "Never, ever do a steak per person," he says. "If you've got something thick, you can have a bit more time to cook it and develop bark — that really gnarly, sumptuous outside." After you get it home, wrap it in parchment paper and stash it in the fridge with a view to eating it within two days. Here's Oliver's favorite method...

1: RENDER THE FAT

Take the steak out of the fridge at least an hour before cooking. Contrary to what you may have been told, oiling and seasoning the raw steak is unnecessary. The animal's fat alone should provide all the oil and flavor you need. "The fat is where you taste the terroir," notes Oliver. To that end, trim off some fat, throw it into a cold pan and put it on to a medium-high heat. Next, add the steak, and hold it fatty-edge down. "You'll see it start to melt like a candle." Wait until the the fatty edge has gone crispy and caramel-colored before turning the steak on its side.

2: PREP THE PEPPER

Flip the steak once every minute. If you don't keep up this frequency, the moisture will rise up through the meat rather than staying in the center. Between flips, take some peppercorns and crush them with a pestle and mortar, then sift them.

"There is a difference in flavor between the outside and the inside of the peppercorn. Sifting them means you can grade out the outer dry husk and just have the essence of pepper." Put this sifted pepper to one side for later.

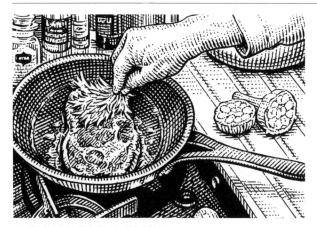

3: ENHANCE THE TASTE

"If you want to introduce some flavors, probably one that could be written into English and Italian religion would be rosemary." Grab a bunch of rosemary sprigs and use them like a paintbrush, dabbing them in the oil of the pan and then on the meat. "Use the rosemary to love the steak."

Another great addition is garlic. Oliver likes to slice a whole bulb in half, rub it all over the meat and then drop the garlic into the pan to cook with the steak. After ten minutes, a steak this thick should, roughly speaking, be medium-rare.

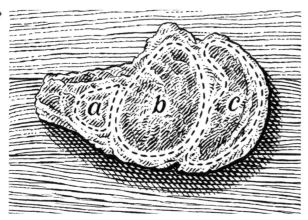

4: WIELD THE KNIFE

Take the steak off the heat and place it in a china dish with the rosemary on top. Let it rest for 5 to 7 minutes before transferring it to a thick, wooden cutting board. Examine the steak: it comprises three separate muscles. Each has a different texture so should be prepared differently. The main eye (b) should be cut into 1cm- (⅜in-) thick slices, the top cap (c) should be diced into rough chunks and the bottom cap (a) sliced thinly, almost like sashimi. Remove any big pieces of fat.

5: SEASON AND SERVE

Sprinkle with some flaky salt from a height, and then do the same with the sieved pepper. "Everyone thinks it's cheffy nonsense, but doing it from a height means it disperses." Next, drizzle the meat with extra virgin olive oil and serve it on the board accompanied by steamed greens and squashed roast potatoes. If you're eating with friends, why not get them involved? "Steaks happen at special times, it's got to be a ceremony," says Oliver. "If you concentrate on the steak, someone musters up a salad and someone else brings a good bottle of wine — then it starts to feel like a thing."

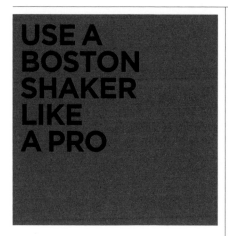

USE A BOSTON SHAKER LIKE A PRO

» In 1806, Frederic Tudor, an enterprising Bostonite, began harvesting ice from the ponds of Massachusetts and shipping it for sale in warmer climes. His idea was met with scorn. "No joke," exclaimed the *Boston Gazette* in February of that year. "A vessel with a cargo of ice has cleared out from this port for Martinique. We hope this will not prove to be a slippery speculation." While the papers scoffed, Tudor had correctly recognized that, in many places outside New England, ice was a sought-after luxury. Over the coming decades, operations such as Tudor's flourished, and ice caught imaginations around the world. In 1840s London, a block of ice was put on display in a shop window on the Strand. "The Londoners look upon it with amazement," a New Englander wrote to a friend back home. As ice became more commonplace, mixed drinks would change forever.

Until then, cocktail recipes had been simple affairs: some spirits, a dash of sugar, perhaps some water and bitters, all stirred together. After bartenders discovered ice, "things started to become more refined," says Agostino Perrone, master mixologist at London's award-winning Connaught Bar. "The function of the ice is not only to chill, but also to allow the mixing process to be more efficient." As cocktails became more complex with ingredients such as eggs and fruit juice, it became necessary to shake rather than simply stir. Hence, the cocktail shaker was born. Its earliest form, which emerged during the mid-nineteenth century, involved two vessels jammed together — a setup that would become known as the Boston. Today, it is the shaker of choice for making long drinks. Here's Perrone's technique...

❯❯ 1: GET THE RIGHT KIT

Buy a Boston shaker comprising two metal tins, rather than a glass-and-tin version. The former is better for several reasons. "I used to work a lot with the glass shaker," recalls Perrone, "but with metal and metal, you chill the drink better and you also don't have the risk of breakages." Put all the ingredients into the smaller tin and fill the larger tin two-thirds of the way up with ice cubes.

2: MAKE IT SECURE

In one motion, pour the liquid over the ice and fit the smaller tin inside the rim of the larger tin. Angle it so that the two tins line up completely straight on one side. On the other side, the tins will form a crescent-moon-shaped cavity.

3: GET A GRIP

Slap the top to make sure it is sealed and pick the whole thing up. Then grip the bottom half in your left hand, with the index and middle fingers on the base, the thumb at the side and the other fingers supporting. The top half should be in your right hand, with the thumb on top and the other fingers supporting.

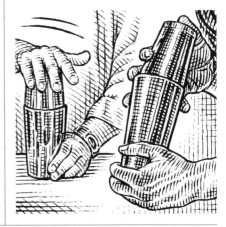

4: SHAKE IT UP

Hold the shaker on its side, straight edge down. Shake it in a figure-of-eight motion. This will ensure you don't smash the ice, which would dilute the drink too much. Note: "If someone is in front of you, always shake away from them in case something... happens." Keep going until the metal feels almost painfully cold, then return it to the bar top. "To open, the secret is to bang it where the crescent-moon gap (*see* step 2) starts." Always keep the index finger on the other side of the upper tin during opening to prevent it from flying off.

5: THE BIT YOU'VE BEEN WAITING FOR

Employ a Hawthorne strainer to retain the ice as you serve the drink. And yes, there's a correct way to do this, too. Hold the tin in one hand and hook your index finger over the top of the strainer, to hold it in place. Pour. Admire. Enjoy.

MASTER SUSHI ETIQUETTE

>> So, you know the difference between sashimi (thin, fresh slices of fish) and nigiri (little parcels of rice topped with raw seafood), and you have learned the basic dos (*do* ask the chef what's best today) and the basic don'ts (*don't* rub your chopsticks together). Yet since the delicacy went global, a host of misconceptions have been perpetuated about how to behave at the sushi bar. We asked Nobu Matsuhisa, the celebrity Japanese chef behind the acclaimed Nobu international chain of restaurants, to advise on the little touches that separate the pros from the pretenders...

1: CHOOSE YOUR WEAPON

If you're eating sashimi, you must use chopsticks. For other types of sushi, fingers are perfectly acceptable. "You can do this the same way you use your chopsticks, but with your thumb and index finger," says Matsuhisa. "Some people don't like to touch the fish — of course, that's OK, they can still use chopsticks."

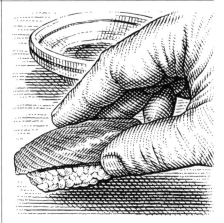

2: RETHINK THE GINGER

No, ginger is not intended as a garnish. "After you have eaten a piece of sushi with tuna, for example, and you want to eat sushi with salmon, you eat the ginger because it cleans the mouth. Then you can try the next piece without confusing the flavors."

3: DIP BUT DON'T DROWN

When eating nigiri, dip it into the soy sauce fish-side first — going rice-first will make the sushi break up. More importantly, use it sparingly. "Otherwise it will just taste of soy sauce rather than the delicate flavors that make the sushi so good. I would recommend you put only a little soy sauce in the dish at a time."

4: FLIP REVERSE

You can place nigiri in your mouth fish-side down. "A lot of the flavor comes from the fish, so it makes sense. But I would not do this if you have also dipped the fish in soy sauce." Note: nigiri is designed to be eaten in one mouthful. "A proper *itamae* (sushi chef) will make it so this is possible."

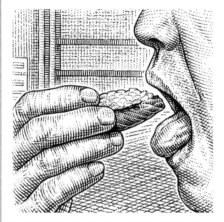

5: HOT TIP

You will likely already have wasabi in your sushi. If you need more, though, place it directly on to the fish with your chopsticks. "Just a small amount, perhaps the size of a pea or less — again, you don't want to just taste the wasabi." But mixing it into your soy sauce? Amateur!

BARBECUE PERFECTLY USING SCIENCE

» A barbecue might seem basic — make fire, add meat, wait a while — but, in truth, it's an art. Its masters flock to contests around the world, one of the most popular being the World Championship that takes place annually in Memphis, Tennessee. Back in 1991, a member of the winning team was Nathan Myhrvold, a Seattle-born foodie who had been devouring cookbooks since his early teens. Myhrvold would go on to train at the famous École de Cuisine La Varenne cooking school in Burgundy — yet he would not become a chef. In fact, he already had a career: he was a scientist.

Myhrvold had earned a doctorate in theoretical and mathematical physics from Princeton University and once spent a year working under Stephen Hawking at Cambridge University. At the time of the barbecue competition he was working as a Vice President for Microsoft, and would later serve as the company's Chief Technology Officer. As the years progressed, however, his two great passions began to converge.

In 2011, Myhrvold released a book, *Modernist Cuisine*. This extraordinary 2,438-page, five-volume encyclopedia draws on years of scientific research to overturn widespread culinary misconceptions and set out the optimum techniques for preparing food. Chef David Chang called it "the cookbook to end all cookbooks." As you might expect, Myhrvold has discovered plenty about barbecues. A crucial point being: contrary to popular belief, it doesn't matter if you cook over charcoal or gas. "There really is not a difference in taste," he tells *GQ*. "There's less romanticism about a gas flame, but it does essentially the same job." Ready to grill? Here are his five hottest tips...

1: GO SHINY OR GO HOME

Crimp aluminium foil around the barbecue's interior. This boosts infrared radiation, which cooks the food. Myhrvold likens the effect of the foil to looking at your reflection in a pair of parallel mirrors. "The food 'sees' infinite copies of the fire," he says. "So the fire seems to extend beyond the edge of the grill." That widens the grill's "sweet spot" where heat is consistent, allowing you to cook your food more evenly.

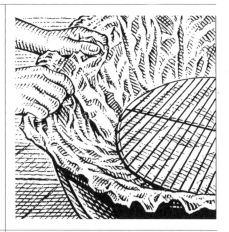

2: PILE IT UP

If you're using charcoal to fuel the barbecue, pile briquettes into a pyramid to maximize their contact with each other. Ignite them with a propane torch, putting the flame to their tapered edges to help them catch fire faster. This method removes the need for firelighters. "Lighter fluid certainly works," says Myhrvold, "but if you put too much on, you will smell it and taste it in the food." Once the coals have whitened, rake them out to form an even layer.

3: TOWEL IT DOWN

It's time to cook. Pat the food dry first. "If the outside of your food has got water on it, you will expend a lot of energy evaporating that water." If that sounds fussy, Myhrvold notes a classic science demonstration in which a wet hand is plunged into a cauldron of molten lead and withdrawn without burns, despite the 600°C (1,112°F) temperatures. "The reason that works is the water takes a huge amount of heat to vaporize."

❯❯ 4: FAT IS YOUR FRIEND

Cooking lean meat or vegetables? Place them near fatty meat because the "barbecue" taste comes from fat dripping on to the coals and flaring (the idea that coals in themselves produce flavor is a major misconception). If there is no fatty meat on hand, simply spray on some clarified butter. "You could squirt a little directly on to the fire," says Myhrvold, "though the advantage of putting it on to the food is that it will drip more slowly on to the coals."

5: USE A HAIRDRYER. NO, REALLY

For thick meat such as steak, first blow a hairdryer through the barbecue's vents until the coals are red hot. Next, sear the steaks on the grill, before putting them in a pan and finishing in a low-heat oven. "That sounds boring, but if you like your steak something other than cremated, it's the best way to do it," says Myhrvold. Use a meat thermometer to work out when it's ready. For steak, very rare is 50°C (122°F); rare is 52°C (126°F); medium-rare is 55°C (131°F); and medium is 60°C (140°F). "Above that," says Myhrvold, laughing, "you shouldn't be doing it."

CHOP AS FAST AS A CHEF

>> It's all very well having expensive kit or fine ingredients, but you'll never excel as a cook without one vital skill. "Having control over your knives is crucial at the high end of the game," says Jason Atherton. A Michelin-starred chef and TV regular, Atherton is the man behind Pollen Street Social in London and 15 other restaurants worldwide. Investing in one decent blade, he says, will take you far. "You need a 20–3cm (8–9-in) all-purpose cook's knife, with about ten percent flexibility in the metal." The first thing to master is chopping vegetables. Here's how to do that at a professional pace…

1: GET TO GRIPS

Hold the handle firmly, with your middle and ring fingers pointing into the palm and the thumb on the side. The index finger should lie on top for weight and control. "Then I can slice the knife underneath something or guide it over the top," says Atherton, "and it's that finger that's doing all the action."

2: ON GUARD

Steady the food in the "claw" grip, as shown, without touching the board. Tuck your fingertips out of harm's way. For larger vegetables, keep two knuckles out in front; for something slimmer and rounder, such as a zucchini, use just one knuckle because, Atherton notes, "you need extra support from your fingers."

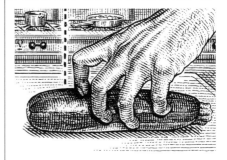

» 3: CHOP CHOP

Hold the blade against the middle bone of the front finger(s) – this is your guard. To slice, move the knife as if the handle is attached to a small wheel rotating toward you, so it slices forward through the food on each stroke. "The tip of the blade should stay in contact with the board throughout the process."

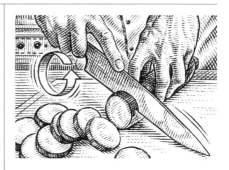

4: THE SPIDER CRAWL

Slide your fingers back toward your wrist as you chop, keeping your thumb static and the blade slicing against your knuckle. When your fingers are too bunched up to continue chopping, keep the knuckle in place but move the thumb back, then the rest of your hand ("like a spider") and start over.

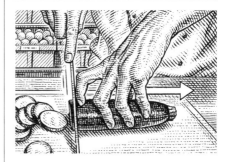

5: PUSH OFF

When you're done, typically there will be pieces of vegetable stuck to the metal. It's tempting to swipe these away with a stroke of your finger. Bad idea. "Just push them off, away from the edge of the blade, with your thumb. Don't ever run your finger down the blade — my gosh!"

SERVE COFFEE THAT'S A WORK OF ART

>> In 1992, Seattle's celebrated café Espresso Vivace began serving lattes with a "rosetta" leaf design drawn in the foam. It would become a staple of "latte art," a catch-all term for such embellishments, which slowly caught on around the globe. One master of the form is Marco Arrigo. He encourages budding baristas to learn latte art because it necessitates pouring the milk at just the right speed. The Head of Quality for coffee brand illy, Arrigo opened London's University of Coffee in 2008 — oh, and he once worked at Espresso Vivace. Here are his steps to the ideal rosetta...

1: GOT MILK?

Prepare some decent espresso: nice and thick, with a serious *crema* (the tawny emulsion that sits on top of the coffee). Next, fill a medium-sized metal jug with milk to the base of the spout. "Then the spout can let me measure how much foam I'm making," explains Arrigo.

2: STEAM POWER

Insert the steam nozzle near the edge of the jug, 2–3mm (^{1}/10 in) below the surface. Hold the jug at a slight angle so that a whirlpool forms, sucking in air. Slowly lower the jug as the milk bubbles rise. Allow the foam to climb about halfway up the spout.

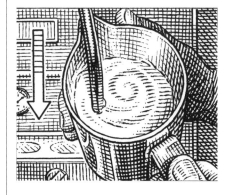

3: THE SWIRL-AND-BANG

It's time to create the velvety milk
"microfoam" required for drawing an
image. Swirl the jug for two seconds and
bang the base on the work surface. Repeat
this twice. Pour away the top layer
of larger bubbles — the layer below will be
the microfoam.

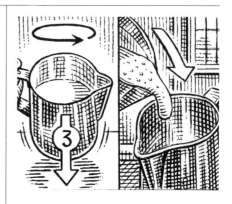

4: TIP YOUR HAND

Grip the jug loosely with your thumb, index,
middle and ring fingers. Hold the base
directly above the cup and pivot from this
position to pour milk into the center of the
cup. This angle forces you to maintain a
higher speed than feels comfortable.

5: ART ATTACK

When the cup is half-full, move the milk
stream to the far edge. Then work back
toward yourself, swinging the jug from
side to side in increasingly smaller strokes.
Now you have the rosetta's leaves. Move
the stream quickly in the other direction
to draw a stem up the center.

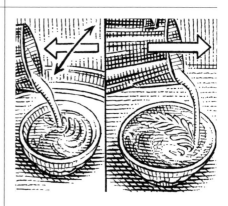

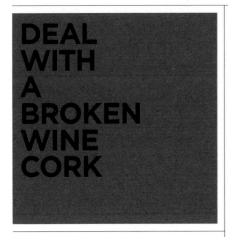

DEAL WITH A BROKEN WINE CORK

>> A broken or disintegrating cork doesn't mean that your wine is "corked." It's a common misconception, but "corking," in fact, refers to a damp taste produced by a naturally occurring chemical compound called TCA. When a bottle's cork is crumbling, the wine inside may actually be perfectly good. The onus is on you to rescue it. Giovanni Ferlito is Head of Wine and Beverage at The Ritz in London, which has a wine list of more than 800 bottles. For him, dealing with failed corks is par for the course — he simply uses the following methods. "All these techniques might happen in the restaurant right in front of you, but you will not notice because the sommelier will do it quite quickly..."

1: REMOVE YOUR CORKSCREW

As soon as you feel a cork start to give — as if you're turning the corkscrew into butter — stop immediately and carefully untwist it. Don't worry, you haven't done anything wrong; the cork is to blame. Often old age will have caused it to perish, though young corks can also degrade if they are too absorbent. "Another reason could be because the bottle has been stored standing up. It's very important when we store wine for the bottle to be laid down so the cork touches the wine and doesn't dry out."

2: MAKE A JUDGMENT

If it's not a particularly expensive bottle, or if you break the cork in the process of trying to pull it out, you may wish to try again to remove it with the corkscrew. "Do not screw in at the same place where you screwed before, because that part is already weak."

Instead, angle the corkscrew at 45 degrees, and wind it into the cork gently. Pull the cork until you can reach it with your fingers. Once you can grip the cork tightly, ease it out. "With your fingers you have much more sensitivity than with the corkscrew."

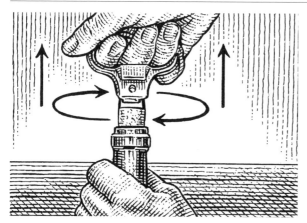

3: CORKSCREW NO GOOD? USE A TWO-PRONG CORK PULLER

This device is the cleanest, most reliable way to remove a bad cork. It is readily and cheaply available, but needs to be handled correctly. Slide the longer prong between the cork and glass, inserting it at the point furthest away from you. Slip the shorter prong in at the nearest edge of the cork.

Flex the handle forward and backward, applying a little pressure each time to carefully work the instrument downward. "The two prongs are now holding the cork very tightly." Simultaneously twist and pull to remove the cork. *Voilà*.

4: NO CORK PULLER ON HAND? SIMPLY PUSH AND POUR

In the absence of a two-prong cork puller, your best bet is to push the cork down into the bottle with a wooden spoon or your finger. "You don't want the cork to stay in the wine for too long, especially because the broken cork parts are quite fresh, so you're going to decant the wine." Line a funnel with a coffee filter or a clean and odorless piece of fine cloth, such as muslin. Insert a long implement, such as a cocktail stirrer into the opening of the bottle, to stop the cork blocking the neck. Decant the wine.

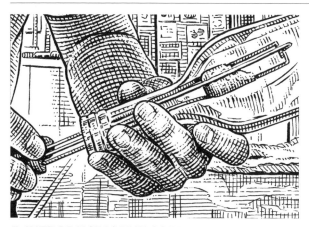

5: INTRODUCING THE CORK RETRIEVER

So, you have pushed in the cork and decanted your wine — but what if you wish to present it in the original bottle? You'll need a cork retriever. Slide it into the bottle and shake the cork into position between the wires. Move the retriever's collar up its wires to pincer the cork. This may take a few attempts: "I have to be honest," says Ferlito, "it's not the easiest!" Twist and pull firmly to remove the cork, then wash the bottle out and allow it to dry upside down. Decant the wine back into the bottle through a filter. Your 1995 Pétrus can now be served in the manner it deserves.

CRACK AN EGG ONE-HANDED

>> Having a date over for dinner is a big play. Not only do you have to serve up something excellent but, let's be candid, you have to look stylish in the process. The culinary move with the greatest panache? Easily the one-handed egg crack. There's a training method that has become quietly standardized among those inclined to learn the technique, and it goes like this...

1: GET SOME BALLS
Practice with two ping-pong balls. Hold them as shown.

2: IT'S IN YOUR GRASP
Pincer a coin between the balls. Rehearse holding then releasing it.

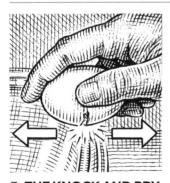

3: THE KNOCK AND PRY
Graduate to an egg. Crack it on a bowl and separate the shell using the motion above.

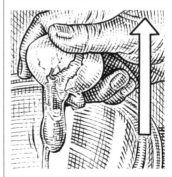

4: SNAP AWAY
As the yolk slides out, rapidly move your hand upward to help the rest on its way.

MIX A MARTINI LIKE THE WORLD'S BEST BARTENDER

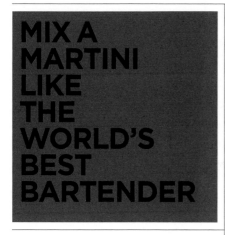

» In Ernest Hemingway's *A Farewell to Arms* (1929), the protagonist drinks a series of Martinis and declares: "I had never tasted anything so cool and clean. They made me feel civilized." This is exactly the desired effect, which is why it's a shame that one of its most common variants, the olive-infused "dirty Martini," often tastes grubby. But that's not the fault of the drink, that's the fault of the bartender.

A man who knows how to make it properly is Erik Lorincz, who runs the American Bar at The Savoy Hotel in London. Not only was the place crowned "Best Bar in the World" by the World's 50 Best Bar awards in 2017, but Lorincz also trained the bartenders who served James Bond his dirty Martini in *Spectre* (2015). Here's how to make 007's cocktail...

1: AVOID THE BIG MISTAKE

The difference between a decent dirty Martini and one that's undrinkable comes down to how you get the olive juice. "Most bartenders use the brine from the olive jar," says Lorincz. This is a no-no. Instead, drop four green olives into the base of a three-piece cocktail shaker.

Lorincz likes to use the Nocellara del Belice olive variety from Sicily. "They are not too salty, with a soft and light vegetable taste and good texture." Crush them with a muddler to extract their flavor.

2: BREAK THE ICE

Use a kitchen towel to hold a block of cloudless ice steady on a cutting board (though more experienced bartenders hold it in their hand) and hack off cubes. Fill the shaker two-thirds full with ice. Why cloudless ice? "It has no bubbles," explains Lorincz, "so the dilution is slower." Cloudless ice can be bought online, or you can make it. First, fill an insulated cooler with water (but don't put a lid on it) and place it in a chest freezer. After four days, remove the box. Once the ice has slightly melted, tip out a clear block.

3: VITAL INGREDIENTS

Measure out 60ml (2oz) of vodka and 15ml (½oz) of dry vermouth (if you're making larger quantities, stick to this 4:1 ratio), and pour it over the ice. Lorincz uses Belvedere for the vodka and Cocchi for the vermouth but notes that, because of the olives, "in a dirty Martini you lose some of the flavor of the spirits."

4: SHAKEN NOT STIRRED

Cradle the shaker horizontally in your right hand, top towards you. Brace it with your left, placing your thumb on the lid. Shake it back and forth vigorously, moving it up and down from chest to head level as you do so. Listen to the sound of the ice. "The longer you shake it, the softer the ice, like going from having stones in the shaker to having sand in the shaker." When you hear the latter sound — usually after about 15 seconds — it's done.

5: TAKE THE STRAIN

Strain into a chilled 190ml (6½oz) Martini glass, shaking the mixer rapidly from side to side to get the liquid out quickly. If you want a drink without tiny pieces of olive in it, you should strain it through a sieve. Finally, add garnish. "Normally we use just one olive, which we drop into the glass." Feel civilized.

2:

FRIENDS & LOVERS

Human interactions aren't chess games. They're messy things, driven by instinct and emotions, and played out within invisible systems of power dynamics. But you can still improve your ability to negotiate your relationships if you drill down on the kind of manageable specifics that you'll find in this chapter. There are strategies for detecting a lie, flirting successfully and winning an argument that will immediately put you on the front foot. And where there are rules, it pays to master them. If you've ever struggled over hosting a dinner party or buying flowers, struggle no more...

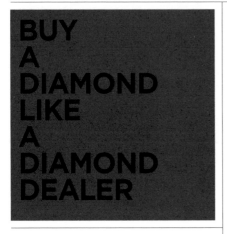

BUY A DIAMOND LIKE A DIAMOND DEALER

»» So you're planning on proposing. Congratulations! Also: beware. The diamond market is murky, full of up-selling, half-truths and retail myths. Take the "rule" dictating that you must spend two months' salary on an engagement ring. That was a clever piece of marketing dreamed up in the Eighties by the gemstone giant De Beers. Customers are now starting to realize, correctly, that you should spend simply what you can afford, but it's obviously important to get the best for your budget. The first step is to give the big brands a swerve — you'll likely save considerably if you ask an independent jeweler to source the stones and make a ring for you. The second is to heed this straight-talking advice from Jessica Elliott, associate jewelry specialist at Christie's auction house...

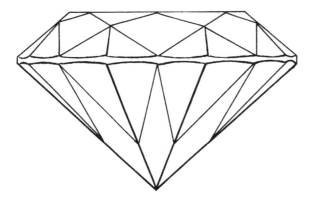

1: IT'S ALL IN THE CUT

The first thing to get right is the cut, as this is what determines sparkle. The "modern round brilliant" is the most desirable — and for good reason. "They standardized this cut in the Twenties," explains Elliott. "Every facet, every angle is within a certain set of parameters so that every single bit of light entering the top of the stone is then returned out to your eye." The quality of a stone's cut (how closely it adheres to ideal proportions) will determine how sparkly it looks. On the GIA certificate that often comes with a stone (*see* step 4), this will be graded from "excellent" to "poor." Never go below "good."

2: GET CLEVER WITH CARATS

A stone's "carat" is its weight, and prices jump at sought-after weight boundaries. "If you want the look of a two-carat stone, you can get a 1.99 and it will cost much less," says Elliott. On the other hand, if you want the prestige of a certain carat level, it's worth buying with a weight margin above the boundary. That's because if you chip the stone and it needs to be repolished (yes, diamonds can be chipped), it's unlikely to fall into a lower weight class and lose disproportionate value.

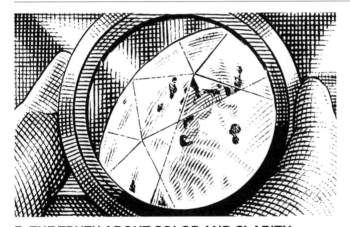

3: THE TRUTH ABOUT COLOR AND CLARITY

Color is graded alphabetically from Z (yellow) to D (colorless); clarity is defined on a scale of 11 esoterically named categories from I3 ("included" — inclusions being flaws) to FL ("flawless"). Each step up is a jump in price. However, to the naked eye, anything above H color will look as good as D, and most stones above VS2 ("very slightly included") will seem clear. Sometimes, you can even go lower in the clarity scale. "Think about the positioning of the inclusion in the stone," advises Elliott. "If it's right on the corner, you could hide it under the claw of the ring setting."

4: GET CERTIFIED

Make sure an expensive stone comes with a certificate from the Gemological Institute of America (GIA) to guarantee that its specs are what the seller claims. "The GIA is the gold standard." As the cost of the process is factored into the overall price of the stone, you may not deem a certificate necessary for a smaller diamond, unless you're paying for very high quality. How to be certain that a certificate relates to your diamond? It will list the carat to two decimal places; have your stone weighed for reassurance.

5: A NOTE ABOUT FLUORESCENCE

Fluorescence devalues a stone. In D to G colors, "medium" to "very strong" fluorescence (in GIA terms) can make the stone appear milky in daylight. However, Elliott notes that if you've had to opt for a colour lower down the scale, fluorescence can actually help. "It can cause a subtle blue glow that can make a yellowish stone look better." Tip: asking about fluorescence is a good way to show expertise, deterring sellers from attempting to overcharge. A similar trick is to ask for details on any inclusions: "Is it a 'crystal,' a 'feather,' a 'pinpoint'...?" Now they know not to mess.

DANCE WITHOUT LOOKING LIKE YOUR DAD

>> They say dancing is like dreaming with your feet. For the rhythmically challenged, it's a waking nightmare. The good news is that you don't have to learn much to look proficient. "With social dancing, less is more," says John Graham, a hip-hop specialist who has worked with the likes of Beyoncé, Rihanna and Justin Bieber, and now teaches at London's Pineapple Dance Studios. Confidence is key, he says, so avoid clamping your arms to your sides — it not only looks as if you're nervous but also inhibits natural movement. No need to go crazy: just keep the arms loose, keep them moving and occasionally snap your fingers to the beat. As for the feet? We asked Graham for five foolproof moves to pull out next time you're on the dance floor...

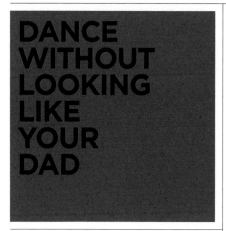

1: THE BOUNCE

Position your feet hip-width apart and soften your knees. Bounce gently up and down in rhythm to the music. Got that? Change it up with a regular bounce on one beat, a bounce with a back-left lean on the next, then a regular bounce again. Then repeat — but with a back-right lean this time — and loop the sequence. "You find this move in most street dance styles," notes Graham. "But you would equate it more with hip-hop."

2: THE TWO-STEP

Slide your left foot sideways on the first beat, slide the other to meet it on the second, then simply repeat in the other direction. That's the simple version of the move. You can add some groove by bouncing with each beat, and leaning in the opposite direction when you slide. Pace-wise, Graham advises imagining you're moving through water. "You know the resistance when you swim? It's got that kind of slow-motion feel, as opposed to staccato."

3: THE ROCKSTEADY

This is all in the hips: rock your right hip outward twice, then your left hip outward twice. Once you're familiar with that, add a "dip" on the second hip rock of each pairing. This means bending your knees and pushing your pelvis backward as the hip is inbound, and straightening up as the hip comes back out again. Repeat on the other side. To finesse this disco staple, twist your torso to the right as you rock your hip to the left side and vice versa.

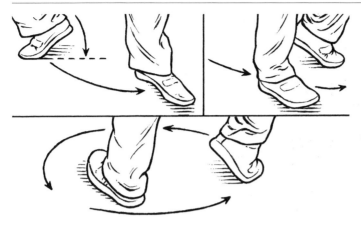

4: THE GLIDE

Stand on the ball of the right foot and heel of the left. Switch the right on to its heel as you slide the left foot out to the left. Shift up on to the ball of the left as it lands in place and slide the right foot in on its heel, pushing past the left, turning your body 180 degrees and pushing the right up on its ball. At this moment, drop the left foot on to its heel and repeat the whole sequence. "You can just keep doing it around the spot that you are on," suggests Graham.

5: A ONE-TIME FLOURISH

Soften your knees and kick out your left leg then your right leg, while staying on the spot. Next, jump, turning 90 degrees counterclockwise and crossing the left leg behind the right as you land. Spin counterclockwise on the ball of the left foot and heel of the right simultaneously, bringing the right foot around to meet the left. You're now facing forward again and ready to keep dancing. Oh, there's a sixth move we forgot to mention: smile.

GIVE A KILLER FOOT MASSAGE

>> When superstar musicians need a massage, they call Dot Stein. She started as a teenager giving back rubs to Def Leppard in exchange for free concert tickets, and word of her talents slowly spread throughout the industry. Eventually Charlie Watts, drummer with The Rolling Stones, insisted he pay for his session and she decided to train professionally. Today, Dr. Dot (a moniker given to her by Frank Zappa) lists everyone from Kanye West to Sting via Gwen Stefani on her list of satisfied customers. One of her specialisms is foot massage. So, the big question: what's the secret to not tickling? "You have to enforce a firm grip from the outset," she says. For your partner's benefit, here is her routine. She recommends repeating each move no fewer than three times...

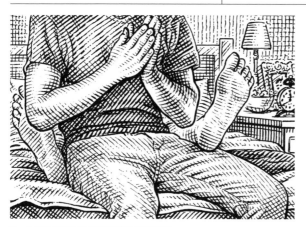

1: ASSUME THE POSITION

Ask your partner to lie down with their feet just off the end of the bed. "A lot of people won't relax because they're afraid their feet stink," says Stein. "So use a nice hot, wet towel to rinse the person's feet." Sit in between their legs, facing away from them with your feet on the ground. If you're starting with their left foot, place it on to your left thigh. Next, warm up a little massage oil in your hands. "Or, if you're at home and you're in a pinch, you can use olive oil, you can use walnut oil, you can use rapeseed oil."

2: DOWN AT HEEL

Interlace the fingers of your two hands. Squeeze their heel between your palms ("It's a really good feeling just to have someone squish your heel") and then do the same to their toes. Next, separate your hands and place a palm against the sole of their foot to "hold hands" with their toes. Move up and down their toes with your fingers, so that you're massaging them all simultaneously.

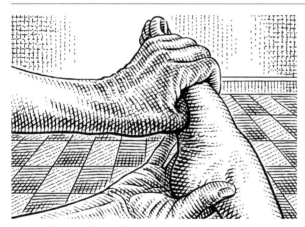

3: MAKE LIKE A LOBSTER

Curl your thumb toward your palm so that your hand resembles a lobster claw. Put all four fingers on the top of the foot, and the lower, larger thumb knuckle into the arch, supporting the heel with your other hand. "It should feel to them like you're using a wooden tool to get way up in there."

Next, brace your four fingers against the outside of the foot and drag that thumb knuckle toward your fingers from the inner arch to the outer. To change it up, "hold hands" again with the toes and work the smaller thumb knuckle up and down between the foot bones.

4: GET TOUGH (IN A GOOD WAY)

Place all four fingers on the outside of the heel. Take the smaller knuckle of the thumb and grind it around the edge of the heel. Next, brace the thumb on the side and work the larger knuckle of the index finger into the heel's center — this puts pressure on the plantar fascia tissue, which produces a sensation in the sweet spot between pleasure and pain.

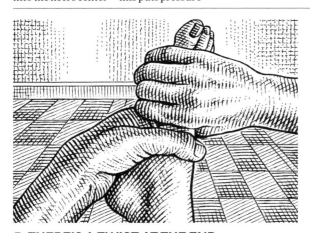

5: THERE'S A TWIST AT THE END

Apply a little more oil and place both your hands around the foot, one above the other as if wringing out a towel. Move one hand clockwise and the other counterclockwise. Work up from the ankle all the way to the toes, building in some thumb action on the sole of the foot. "Nothing feels better."

To finish off the massage, take a soft cloth and give each toe a tug. "Not a fast, violent tug but slow and hard — you can feel the toes crack usually. And that's very relieving."

FIND OUT IF SOMEONE'S LYING TO YOU

>> Lies are everywhere. According to Pamela Meyer, the author of *Liespotting* (2010), you can expect to be on the receiving end of between ten and 200 lies per day, from white lies to more serious deceits. There's a widespread perception that spotting a lie is a matter of intuition, but Meyer is an expert in its science. Her deception detection techniques are so effective that her company Calibrate consults widely for governmental bodies and private companies, such as hedge funds and law firms. She has developed an effective conversational strategy to get to the truth, which can be broken down to an acronym: B.A.S.I.C. If you are suspicious that an acquaintance is lying to you about something serious and you want to confront them, here's how to go about it...

1: B(ASELINE)

Study the baseline behavior of the person in question, so you can assess divergence from the norm. "If someone's tapping their foot when you ask them a question, it doesn't mean anything unless they're normally very calm," says Meyer. Observe their laugh, gestures and facial reactions — but, most importantly, gauge their vocal tone, speed and pitch, and check out their posture. Voice and posture tend to change the most when someone is lying. Take special note of any tics, so you don't misinterpret them as "tells" later.

2: A(SK OPEN-ENDED QUESTIONS)

Time to interrogate. Choose a location that is quiet, relaxed and with a visible exit, then start a conversation. Ask open-ended questions to avoid sounding accusatory, slowly narrowing them down to get at the information you want. Never ask, "Why?"

Instead, ask, "What made you do that?" as it implies they had a legitimate reason. The end phase is to propose stories that rationalize what the person might have done — this makes it more likely that they'll be honest.

3: S(TUDY CLUSTERS)

As they reply to your more specific questions, look for clusters of verbal and non-verbal signs of duplicity that diverge from the baseline. Verbals include distancing language and repeating questions to stall for time; non-verbals include freezing the upper body, pursed lips, fake smiles and

post-interview relief. You need to "raise the cognitive load" in order to cause these signs to leak out — get them to tell their story backward, or give them new information, such as the fact that you have a witness. Ultimately, ask yourself if they shifted from being cooperative to being evasive.

4: I(NTUIT THE GAPS)

Look out for "gaps" in what they're saying. These could be emotional gaps (they say they're concerned but their facial expression suggests the opposite), factual gaps between their account and the evidence, behavioral gaps between how they claim to have acted and their normal habits, or logical gaps in the story. Your gut can be good for spotting emotional gaps, but often the most useful analysis is simply comparing how somebody describes a chain of events versus how they logically would have unfolded.

5: C(ONFIRM)

If you believe someone is lying, test your hunch with confirmation questions. "Often we start with, 'How do you feel about this accusation?' Someone who's guilty will blather on in a completely odd way, expressing many different kinds of emotions." An innocent person, however, will typically be angry about being falsely accused. Another approach is to ask what the consequences should be for the alleged misdemeanor. "Almost universally, a guilty person would recommend leniency."

FINESSE YOUR FLIRTING

>> Animals have it easy. When they want to attract a mate, they let out a call that leaves no doubt as to their intentions. For humans, the language of attraction is more ambiguous. While some people are naturally literate in its signs and codes, for others it can seem as inscrutable as Ancient Greek. So how do you send the right signal? And how do you avoid awkwardness or, worse, creepiness? Those questions intrigue Jean Smith. The social and cultural anthropologist conducted 250 interviews with people in London, Paris, New York and Stockholm to investigate flirting behaviors, publishing her expertise in books such as *The Flirt Interpreter* (2012) and, later, *Flirtology* (2018). Since she also coaches flirting through events such as TEDx and her business, Flirtology, we asked for a tutorial...

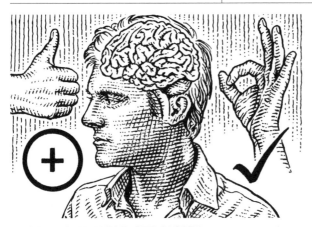

1: GET YOUR HEAD STRAIGHT

The biggest inhibitor to successful flirting is being too frightened to flirt in the first place. It's crucial to adopt what Smith calls "mental models" to neutralize anxieties. So: are you afraid of rejection? Don't see flirting as a test of your personality ("That *would* make you scared of rejection"). The mental model should simply be "let's have fun" — think of it that way and it takes the pressure off. Another useful mental model, if you are nervous about approaching a stranger, is "don't hesitate, just go."

2: TAKE THE PLUNGE

Someone has caught your attention. Should you approach? The most important test is eye contact. If it happens multiple times, if they hold your gaze and if it's accompanied by a small gesture, such as adjusting their clothes, those are good signs. Smile and walk over. Next, stop worrying about your opening line. Smith says that "What do you think of X?" where X is relevant to something you are both experiencing — the music, a painting — is perfectly good. "It's already starting to create the 'us,' and it's open-ended."

3: BUILD ON IT

They didn't blow you off, so now you build rapport. Successful rapport, according to Smith, involves self-disclosure and finding commonalities. Topics should be light, and you need to tread the line between asking and answering questions. If you've done either more than three consecutive times, there's an imbalance. The most important thing, though? This isn't yet the flirting stage. This is the moment where if you're getting a lukewarm response — if they aren't engaging — you make an exit. Otherwise you're being a creep.

4: FLIRT AWAY

Smith has identified six aspects of flirting. She uses an acronym: H.O.T. A.P.E. That stands for Humour, Open body language, Touch, Attention, Proximity and Eye contact. The most nuanced is touch. "Touch is wonderful, but you have to make sure the other person is respondent. Don't use it to 'create' attraction." If signs are good, Smith recommends briefly tapping the side of their hand as you make a comment. A good indicator that it's going well is if their feet and shoulders are pointing straight at you.

5: THE END GAME

When the encounter comes to an end, you'll need to show your hand about seeing them again. It's best to be as direct as possible — a strategy that in itself may make you more attractive to them. But what exactly should you say? "You just link it to whatever you've been talking about. If you're talking about food, such as Italian, you could say, 'Hey, why don't I take you to my favorite Italian restaurant?' Or it could even be, 'I haven't had a conversation this interesting in so long, do you want to meet up again over a glass of wine and we can continue this?'"

THROW A FORMAL DINNER PARTY

>> In the Eighties and Nineties, the dinner party was in its prime: bombastic, dressed up, four-coursed and late-finishing. Then, as the 2000s crept in, it was unceremoniously edged out. The restaurant scene was reimagined as youth culture, as a new kind of indie rock, with the effect that trying the latest tasting room/nouveau burger joint/artisanal mocktail list became the thing. Entertaining at home was predominantly about hosting kitchen suppers, an outwardly more casual affair — even if hosts actually cared deeply about everyone admiring their culinary handiwork and, of course, their kitchen. But for every action there's a reaction. Of late, the dinner party has made a bullish comeback, in all its former (and formal) glory. Here's *GQ* Editor Dylan Jones's advice on hosting one...

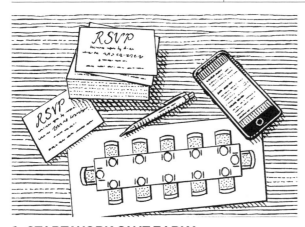

1: START WORK ON IT EARLY

Invite guests either by phone or printed card at least three weeks before the event. If you need to replace someone who has pulled out, you can extend a last-minute invitation, but don't allow one friend to become your default stand-in. Always do a *placement* dinner: stick to the traditional boy-girl-boy-girl template, but mix up couples or close friends with new people. You need easy access to the kitchen, so position yourself accordingly. Maintain the seating arrangement for all of the courses — only then encourage people to switch places.

2: SET THE TABLE IN THE TRADITIONAL MANNER

For each place setting, the starter knife and fork should be on the outside so guests can work inward from there; the dessert fork and spoon should lie across the top as shown. Linen napkins are preferable, but (good-quality) paper napkins are fine.

Provide appropriate glasses for water, red wine, white wine and dessert wine, and arrange these in any order above the knives. A word to the wise: if you get up to leave the table mid-course, the napkin goes on your chair, not on the table.

3: THE FOOD SHOULD BE PRACTICAL, NOT PRETENTIOUS

You need to serve hors d'oeuvres with predinner drinks, if only because this stops your guests getting too drunk. Eighty pieces is about right for 12 people. For the dinner itself, feel free to scour cookbooks for inspiration, but don't cook anything ostentatious or that you're not confident in cooking. Four courses — a starter or salad, main course, cheese and dessert — is *de rigueur*. If your dinner is catered, ask the chefs to prepare dishes that you could feasibly make yourself or it will just seem, well, odd.

4: GIVE THE DRINKS DUE CONSIDERATION

When your guests arrive, either offer them a set drink (champagne, say, or a vodka tonic) or specify a small selection. Pace the refills: people should drink enough to feel relaxed, but not so much that they don't actually enjoy your food. How much wine should you buy? A safe bet is a bottle of red and a bottle of white for each guest. You probably won't get through all that, but it does ensure that you won't run out. Water is best served on the table in bottles (if it's a good brand) or glass jugs (if it's from the tap).

5: DON'T MESS UP THE MUSIC

If you're stuck for what music to put on, here's a simple principle: imagine you're in a restaurant. That may well mean you decide not to play anything. After all, how often has your experience of eating out actually been improved by the music? If you would like some, however, make sure it's instrumental — Sixties film soundtracks, Eighties alt-country and Nineties Japanese loungecore are rich seams — and prepare a playlist ahead of the evening. It should move elegantly between genres and be long enough that it won't repeat itself, otherwise guests will worry that they've outstayed their welcome.

BUY FLOWERS FOR YOUR LOVER

>> When Whitney Bromberg Hawkings was working as Tom Ford's right-hand woman, she witnessed how the world's most stylish people send flowers. She has since parlayed that expertise into FlowerBx, a flower delivery service that is now a go-to in the fashion world. Her client list includes Dior, De Beers, Jimmy Choo and countless celebrities. One thing she has learned is that, for such a small gesture, flowers produce outsized joy. In other words, if you send some to your partner (ideally to their office — everyone loves the attention), they're the gift that gives back...

1: DON'T BUY A MIXED BOUQUET

"When Karl [Lagerfeld] would send Tom [Ford] flowers, when Calvin [Klein] would send Tom flowers — when any of them would — they all sent a massive bunch of one type of flower," says Hawkings. "It looks so pure, so amazing." No need to add foliage or filler, just have them wrapped in brown paper.

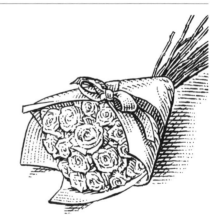

2: CHOOSE A FAIL-SAFE FLOWER

"Each season there is definitely a star." In winter go for ranunculus; in spring, peonies; in summer, dahlias; and in autumn, hydrangeas. Roses are available all year round — but red ones can seem unimaginative. Hawkings prefers pale pink. "It's chicer."

WINTER   SPRING

AUTUMN   SUMMER

3: GIVE THE FLOWERS A HEALTH CHECK

A good bunch of flowers should last more than a few days. Avoid buying anything already in full bloom. "Flowers in bud form are as fresh as you can get them, and that's what you want." Also look at the colors. "If there's any yellowing on the leaves or on the petals, I would stay away."

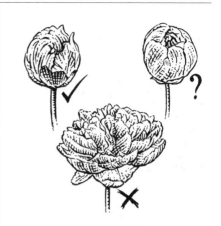

4: MAKE THE ACCOMPANYING NOTE SHORT AND SWEET

"You can't go wrong with 'I love you.' That means the whole world, even if you've been married for 13 years." The same is true for apology flowers. "I had a bad situation a few years ago, and someone wrote on their note 'I'm sorry' and drew a sad face. That's all they needed to say."

5: AND IF YOU CAN'T GET TO A DECENT FLORIST...

If you have to buy from a supermarket, you will need to repackage. At home, "stick them together in a vase, and you're not going to go wrong." If out and about, switch the cellophane for brown paper. Not possible? Buy a potted orchid and remove the packaging. Done.

WIN AN ARGUMENT LIKE A LAWYER

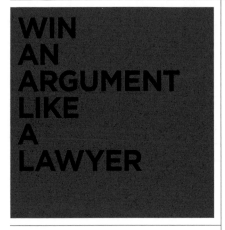

>> If you were to find yourself on the wrong side of the law, you would want Tunde Okewale fighting your corner. Specializing in criminal cases, Okewale works at Doughty Street Chambers in the UK — where Amal Clooney also practices — and has won a fearsome reputation as an advocate. (Don't take it from us: take it from *The Lawyer* magazine, which named him Young Barrister of the Year in 2012.) He also runs Urban Lawyers, which aims to make the law more accessible to marginalized groups — an example of the kind of community work that earned him an MBE in 2016. As if he weren't spinning enough plates, he also practices sports law, representing soccer players, boxers and Olympic athletes. Next time you're embroiled in a debate, channel his advice to emerge victorious...

1: ASK THEM "WHY?"

"Often people don't really want to argue, they just want to be heard," says Okewale. "If you give people an opportunity to express themselves, in many cases it makes them more receptive to your argument." If your subsequent logic is sound, you stand a better chance of winning them over. A similar tactic is asking your opponent to explain their point in step-by-step, cause-to-effect-level detail. Often, in the process, they will realize they don't fully understand what they're advocating, or at least they have to confront the inherent assumptions and prejudices on which they've based their position.

2: CROSS-EXAMINE THEM

Turn the facts that support your case into a series of questions to which your opponent has to say "yes." For instance, if you're arguing that Liverpool is a better soccer team than Arsenal, the questions might be: "Liverpool are higher in the league, correct?"; "Liverpool have scored more goals, correct?"; "Liverpool have spent more money, correct?"; "So, you'd accept that Liverpool are a better team?" They will either have to agree with you or feel ridiculous saying "No."

3: CHALLENGE THE EVIDENCE

If you're arguing with someone who has a good memory, they can have you on the back foot by reeling out statistics that support their argument. The way to deal with this is to challenge the numbers' validity. Ask them what the sample size was, for instance, where the stat came from and how old the study is. "If they don't know the answer, make the point that they can't necessarily rely on the statistic." Equally, if you're using statistics, you should anticipate objections. You might say: "It's true that this is an old sample, however, there is evidence from these places that supports it..."

4: UNPICK LOGICAL FALLACIES

Learn common logical fallacies so you can detect and challenge them. For instance, there's the "correlative fallacy" that a correlation is evidence of causation; the "argument from incredulity" ("I can't believe X is true, so therefore X must be false"), and the "straw man" where your opponent appears to refute your argument while actually attacking a point that you never made. The other benefit of knowing these fallacies is you can then sneakily use them yourself — because they can be convincing.

5: BE PERSUASIVE

"Persuasiveness is something that's often overlooked. Sometimes, even if your logic is faulty, your use of language, tone and voice inflection may be the reason you win an argument." Analogies can be very helpful, as they are visual and introduce a sense of veracity. "I was once trying to convince the jury that although my client lied in interview, when he gave evidence on oath in the witness box, they should still believe him. What I did was recite the folk tale of *The Boy Who Cried Wolf*." That's more convincing than simply, "Just because he lied once, it doesn't mean he will always lie."

BREAK UP WITH SOMEONE THE RIGHT WAY

>> If you're breaking up with someone, there's no need to be cruel or cowardly about it. The aim should be that, when the dust has settled, your partner will look back and respect you for how you did it. If that sounds like a fool's errand, Natalia Juarez would beg to differ. Juarez is the founder of BetterBreakups, a Toronto-based break-up and divorce coaching service that helps people on both sides of the equation: the "dumpees," who need to work through the trauma, and the "dumpers," who aren't sure how to approach the ordeal in the first place.

Juarez says that half the battle of initiating a break-up is admitting to oneself that it's time to call it a day. From her experience, the most common sign of a relationship in crisis is one party feeling an overarching sense of disgust or contempt toward the other. That's because the brain starts fixating on the partner's downsides to find reasons to leave them. "It shows that you have stopped deeply caring about this person and you have lost respect," says Juarez. That's not to say that it is definitely over — if you feel the relationship is worth saving, you need to start talking it through — but if it goes on for too long, then it's hard to repair.

And that's OK. "I really believe that longevity is not an indicator of a successful relationship. Most of us will have a few different long-term relationships in our lives, so learning how to be in a healthy relationship — and to break up in a healthy way — are actually essential skills." To wit...

» 1: DON'T TALK YOURSELF OUT OF DOING IT

Sure, change is frightening and you don't want to hurt the other person — but you need to get past that. Reframe breaking up as a positive. Juarez advises thinking of it like this: "The most loving thing that you can do is to let them go, so that they are able to find someone who truly wants to be with them."

2: GIVE FAIR WARNING

It's traumatic to blindside. "If you're having doubts, you should start introducing these conversations into the relationship." When you do eventually push the button, there's never a good moment but there are less bad ones. Juarez suggests breaking up on a Thursday, because the other person can take the Friday off work, if necessary, and then has the weekend to process everything.

3: LET THEM DOWN GENTLY BUT FIRMLY

Do it at their home or your shared home, having found a place to stay elsewhere. Don't put the blame on them. The tenor should be: "You deserve more, I'm not able to give you what you need, and this is why," and/or "We deserve more, and this is what I feel isn't working about the relationship." Also, let them know when you'll be leaving. This will give them an opportunity to ask questions but also prevent the conversation rolling on.

4: HANDLE THE AFTERMATH

At the end of the break-up conversation, offer to speak to them the following week and warn them that you're going to disconnect on social media (for Juarez, this is essential). You may also need to return each other's possessions. Do this within three to ten days through a neutral friend. "Pack up their stuff nicely and only send back the important things." Returning tea bags, say, is petty.

5: GET OVER IT

It's upsetting for the person getting dumped, but it's not exactly a happy time for you, either. "It's incredibly disorienting and stressful. So start journaling, talking it out, do exercise." How does Juarez feel about rebounds? "It can be a part of processing the break-up. Connecting with someone else can be healing."

3:

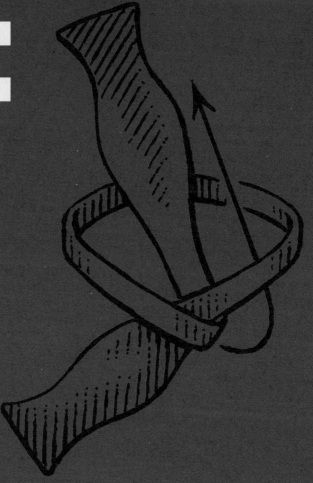

STYLE
SECRETS

GQ started life as *Apparel Arts*, a trade publication for retailers and wholesale buyers in the clothing industry. Unintentionally, it caught on with the general public and, in 1957, re-launched as a consumer title bearing the strapline "Gentlemen's Quarterly." The publisher declared that "its entire editorial content will be devoted to fashion and fashion-related features." Well, today that agenda has grown — we cover everything from music and sport to politics and technology — but style remains our spiritual heartland. In this chapter you'll find insider advice on everything from tying your scarf to advanced shaving techniques...

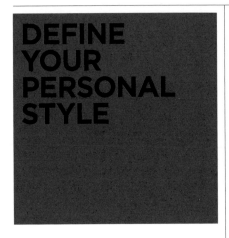

DEFINE YOUR PERSONAL STYLE

>> Successful men often have a signature look. Think about Steve Jobs and his black turtlenecks; Idris Elba and his polo shirts; or Karl Lagerfeld and his dependable black-suit-black-gloves-black-sunglasses combo. It might seem like a quirk (and, let's face it, for Lagerfeld it is), but there can be a practical benefit to dressing predictably. "You'll see I wear only gray or blue suits," President Obama once told *Vanity Fair*. "I'm trying to pare down decisions. I don't want to make decisions about what I'm eating or wearing. Because I have too many other decisions to make."

It can also help with cultivating a personal brand. Appearing too busy to concern oneself with clothing choices suggests status. And the specific style that one settles on can send more subtle messages, besides. Take Mark Zuckerberg's plain gray T-shirts: they telegraph that despite his wealth he's still down to earth, that he's just in it for the science. Or David Gandy's mismatched three-pieces, which announce that he might wear suits, but — let's get this straight — he isn't a "suit."

To develop your own signature wardrobe, there are two guiding principles. First, you need to pick a theme that flatters you. Bluer colors suit lighter skin tones, for instance, whereas warmer hues go better with darker ones. Second, you don't want to emulate a character from *The Simpsons* and wear literally the same thing day in, day out — it's important to have a degree of variety and flexibility. We can't tell you exactly what to wear, but we can give you some tricks to help work it out...

1: KNOW THYSELF

Go through your wardrobe. See those items with the faded colors or the tired-looking fabric? They're your favorites. From that set, pick out staple items that you have worn in the last year, from shoes and jeans to shirts and blazers. Make sure to include a suit.

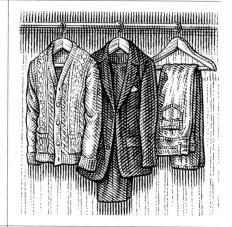

2: MIX AND MATCH

Construct at least three ensembles of varying formality — and ignore trends. The goal is to look timeless. Next, buy multiples of each item (you never know when your favorite jeans cut is going to be discontinued), including an extra pair of pants for the suit. Now you have your base.

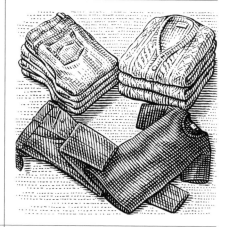

3: GET PERSONAL

Make it your own by adding a twist. Keith Richards has his skull ring, Bob Dylan has his sunglasses, Angelo Galasso wears his watch on his shirt cuff. But you could go for something a little more sober — an elegant bracelet, perhaps, a flower lapel pin or some horn-rimmed glasses.

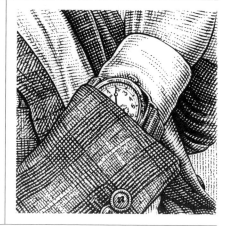

❱❱ 4: GIVE THEM A BREAK

Don't make the mistake of wearing an item to death while keeping its backups pristine. Leather shoes, for example, last longer if they're given time to rest between wears — that's because if they're allowed to dry out properly, they maintain their shape. Cycle through your clothes to reduce overall wear and tear.

5: BREAK YOUR OWN RULES

If a situation requires a dress code that your wardrobe can't provide, it's better to buy the required items than to come off as a chump. So you never wear a tie? Well, at your sister's wedding, guess what? You do.

HANG YOUR PANTS USING THE SAVILE ROW FOLD

>> How often have you gone to put on your carefully pressed suit, only to find that the pants have slipped off the hanger and are now looking decidedly unpressed at the bottom of your wardrobe? The easiest solution comes from Savile Row, home to London's oldest (and greatest) tailors. From time immemorial, they have been using a simple technique to keep customers' pants securely in place without resorting to grips or clips but using friction alone. Here's the secret, so you can do it at home...

1: PREPARE

Fold your pants flat and lay them neatly on the bed.

2: FOLD

Fold the top leg inward over the bar of the hanger.

3: REPEAT

Fold an equal amount of the bottom leg over the top.

4: STASH

Hang the pants in your wardrobe. Take that, gravity!

SPOT A FAKE ROLEX

>> When newbies prepare to start building a watch collection, they often disregard Rolex because its fame makes the brand seem a cliché. They start obsessing over what they perceive as more specialty names, such as Jaeger-LeCoultre or A. Lange & Söhne. But as their expertise grows, they invariably add a Rolex back to their want list — and probably make it their first purchase. Few can match this Geneva-based watchmaker for reliability, durability and innovation. Its timepieces are also relatively affordable in terms of the rarefied world of luxury watches, particularly if you buy a "preowned" model (that's the industry euphemism for "second-hand"). The problem is, of course, that the market is littered with counterfeits — and some of them are worryingly convincing. So how do you know that you're buying the genuine article?

We consulted Adrian Hailwood, former Director of Watches at Fellows auctioneers, a favorite supplier to those in the industry. His overriding piece of advice is straightforward: "You're buying the seller as well as buying the watch. If you're buying from someone who is a bricks-and-mortar operation, who you can physically take it back to, whether it be an auction house or a specialist vintage dealer, they're going to take care of you if there turns out to be a problem." Actual fake-spotting, however, is rather more complicated. There's a myth that forgeries don't have Rolex-style "sweep" second hands — in fact, many do. Instead, you need to examine the finer details. That's why you first need to acquire a loupe, a tiny but powerful jeweler's magnifying glass for getting up close and personal with the timepiece. Here's what to look for...

1: MARK IT OUT

If it's gold, find the hallmarks. One should depict either Helvetia, the female symbol of Switzerland, or a St. Bernard dog. Despite their tiny size, these hallmarks should look "very three-dimensional, and very crisply done," says Hailwood. Sometimes signs of wear can be genuine, but a blurry image should always raise suspicions.

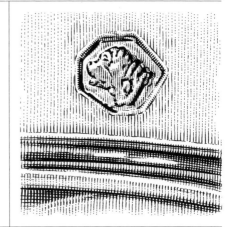

2: GOT ID?

Authenticity documents (whether paper or bankcard-style) help resale value, but can themselves be faked. "When they are, the print quality gives it away: it's a little ragged, a little off-centerd or it's smudged. Most things Rolex do are so crisp, the moment anything deviates from that, you're like, 'Really?'"

3: IT'S WHAT'S ON THE INSIDE THAT COUNTS

"If you were to ask, 'What is the rock-solid test?' I would always say, 'The movement.'" This is the watch's internal mechanism, which the dealer should agree to show you. It ought to be highly polished — even on the sides of its parts — and should exactly match a photo of the real thing.

❯❯ 4: CHECK THE BODYWORK

The bracelet can be a giveaway — if the edges of the links feel sharp, that's wrong. "Fakes aren't machined to feel nice in the hand." Next, ask the dealer to remove the bracelet. Between the lugs at 12 o'clock (*see* picture), there should be a shiny, hand-engraved model number.

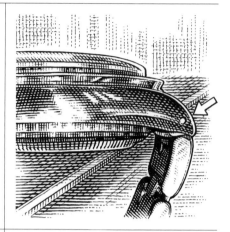

5: DIAL DOWN ON THE DIAL

Some models have an internal serial number — it should be oriented as shown. Elsewhere on the dial, if there is a magnifying window, hold the watch so you see the date unmagnified, then rotate it so the date aligns under the lens. Fakes often magnify just 1.5x rather than 2.5x. "You want to see a real visual 'pop.'"

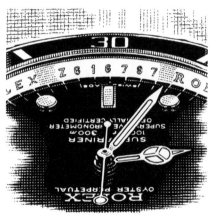

TIE YOUR SCARF IN A GILET KNOT

>> Ah, the humble scarf — so simple yet so problematic. Here at *GQ*, most of the style questions we get asked about scarves concern how to wear them. Is looping and tucking too feminine? Is a drape too pedestrian? And what's the best way to do either anyway? You can understand the anxiety, to a point. When it comes to fashion, men have fewer variables to play with than women, so small things end up commanding disproportionate attention. Well, there's one knot that goes perfectly with a formal overcoat and we love it for its balance of warmth and elegance. We call it "the gilet knot" (or "the kidney warmer")...

1: SCARF UP
Acquire a thin scarf with some length to it. Drape it around your neck, making sure the ends line up.

2: THE PASS
Cross the scarf neatly over your chest, keeping it as flat as possible, and pass it around your sides.

3: SECURE
If it's long enough, simply tie the ends together just above your waistband. If not, tuck the ends into your pants.

4: STEP OUT
Add an elegant overcoat (single-breasted works particularly well) and pop the collar. Voilà: all the warmth of a gilet; all the style of a Parisian.

SPEED-FOLD WITH THE TOKYO T-SHIRT TECHNIQUE

>> The origins of this method for folding a T-shirt quickly and perfectly are hazy. We've seen it used in shops from the UK to the US, but it has become closely associated with Japan. That's thanks to a clip of a woman demonstrating the technique on Japanese television, which has been widely circulated and imitated online. No wonder: it's a nifty life hack, and the best practitioners can do it in under five seconds. Here's how...

1: LAY IT OUT

Place the garment on a level surface, face up and sideways on to you. Make sure its edges are straight and the fabric is perfectly flat.

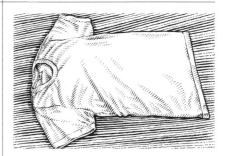

2: FIX YOUR CROSSHAIRS

Envisage a vertical line running exactly up the middle of the garment. Imagine another running horizontally across from the center of the right shoulder seam. Pinch the material with your left hand at the point where the two lines intersect.

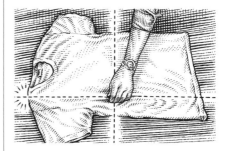

3: HOLD SOME, FOLD SOME

Take the center of the right shoulder seam between the thumb and index finger of your right hand. Cross your right hand over your left, pulling the fabric over, and grab the garment at the other end of that horizontal line.

4: SHAKE IT OUT

Uncross your hands, keeping hold of the material. As you do this, it might seem like it's going wrong, but trust that it isn't. Shake flat.

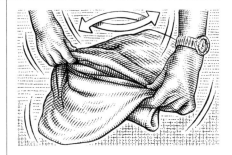

5: THE TUCK

Lower the T-shirt back on to the surface so that the left sleeve tucks underneath. Perfect.

KEEP YOUR SNEAKERS ICY-WHITE

» Consider the most enduring sneaker designs — the Nike Air Force 1, for instance. Launched in 1982, this chunky creation gained such traction outside of its original hip-hop fan base that it has become everyman footwear. Or the Adidas Superstar: originally championed by the NBA pros of the Seventies, it's still seen today on the feet of everyone from Jay-Z to David Beckham. Then there's the ever-popular Converse Chuck Taylor All Star, which began life when the basketball player Chuck Taylor joined a team sponsored by the Converse Company — way back in 1923. And what do all of these timeless shoes have in common? Their signature colorway is mainly white.

That's no coincidence. White sneakers and popularity go hand in hand. Sneakerheads fixate on shoes' silhouettes and the lack of color emphasizes shape. Moreover, it makes them versatile, a kind of sartorial blank canvas that can form the basis of any number of looks, whatever the season or the decade.

The problem is that no matter how watchful you are, white sneakers are practically guaranteed to get dirty eventually — and if you're anything like us, that's irksome. A box-fresh pair of Nike Air Jordans can be worn to the office (if you work in that kind of office), but as soon as they get scuffed, forget it — hell, there are nightclubs that would gladly turn you away. While canvas shoes can be thrown in the washing machine, sneakers with leather or synthetic uppers are more of a challenge to restore to their former icy white glory. But nobody said looking good was easy...

1: LACE WITH BLEACH

Remove the laces and throw them into a bowl of warm water with some detergent and a splash of bleach. Swirl them around and massage the fabric; leave for five minutes. Rinse them in clean water and flatten them out on a piece of paper towel to dry.

2: GIVE IT THE BRUSH-OFF

Wipe down the shoes with a damp cloth, and use a toothbrush to get dirt out of nooks and crannies. Your local supermarket will sell stain-removal scrubber pads — these are meant for household cleaning but are also great for getting marks off the edges of the soles.

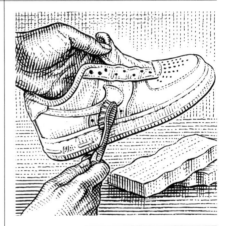

3: BUBBLE OVER

Visit a dedicated sneaker store and buy some specialty cleaner — or, failing that, simply use regular dishwashing liquid. Squirt this on to a clean shoebrush, dunk the brush in hot water and work up a lather on the shoe's upper. Note: any suede areas will require softer bristles.

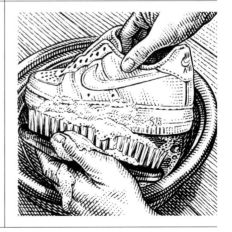

❯❯ 4: DRY-CLEAN

Rinse off the soap under a warm tap.
Next, use a microfiber cloth to gently dry
the shoes. If there are stubborn marks, you
may have to rub harder but be careful not
to cause damage. Only apply real force on
robust areas, such as the sole or toecap.

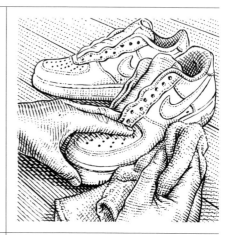

5: ON YOUR GUARD

Spray with a specialty sneaker protector for
stain resistance. If you're wearing new jeans,
put duct tape inside the leg cuff to prevent
dye bleeding on to the leather. You might call
that obsessive; we'd say it's conscientious.

DEPLOY THE MILITARY TUCK

» There are few things more inelegant than a billowy shirt. So when we heard that American soldiers have an unofficial method to keep theirs looking presentable, we did a little research. The US Marine Corps generally wear elasticated "shirt stays" when they need to look their best — but it turns out that when these aren't available, or the situation doesn't demand such fastidiousness, they use the time-honored technique set out here. Caveat: if your shirt is so baggy it looks like a collapsed soufflé, then you simply need to buy one in a slimmer fit. Shirt sorted? Read on...

1: PANTS UP

Tuck in the front of the shirt. Zip up your fly but do not button.

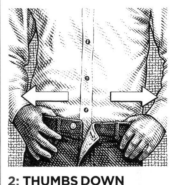

2: THUMBS DOWN

Move your thumbs around your waistband from front to back, tucking in the shirt.

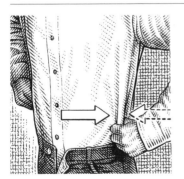

3: PLEAT IT

At the 4 and 8 o'clock positions, fold the excess into pleats.

4: FINE-TUNE

Button your pants and tidy up as required. Carry on.

SHAVE WITH NEXT-LEVEL RAZOR SKILLS

» We'll let you in on a secret: there's a whole set of wet-shaving strokes out there that your father never taught you. While the standard "slide razor down face" approach will usually do a better job of getting rid of your stubble than an electric razor, it will never quite remove everything. Enter the shaving geeks, a community of tinkerers first brought together by web forums in the Nineties, who have developed a set of advanced techniques. One of their most high-profile figures is Texas-based Mark Herro, who runs the blog Sharpologist.com. We asked him for some face-enhancing moves...

1: PREP THE FLESH

Before you try the two techniques below, you should remove the bulk of your stubble. The best way is with the "Gillette slide," whereby you move the razor diagonally downward while keeping it horizontal. "It approaches the hair at a more efficient angle," says Herro. "Like a guillotine."

2: GET TO GRIPS

In preparation for the "J-hook" (see step 3), re-lather, then shift your razor grip so you're holding the end of the handle lightly by your fingertips. Indeed, with all shaving, lightness is key. "Otherwise, if you press down hard, the skin ripples and the blade edge cannot maintain a consistent contact."

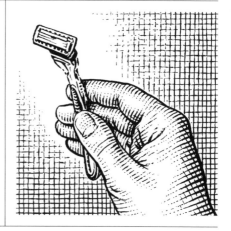

3: INTRODUCING THE "J-HOOK"

For areas of awkward grain variation, move the blade in small "J" motions. "Think of it like a golf swing. So you're starting a stroke before the area you want to use the J-hook on, and as you approach that area you do the J-turn and follow through."

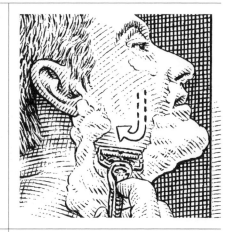

4: CHANGE IT UP

Where grain dictates, shift the J-hook on its side. "The J-hook looked so scary when I first saw it, I did not try it for six months. But after I did, I realized it wasn't difficult. I have come to rely on it fairly routinely to clean up little bits of stubble on my neck."

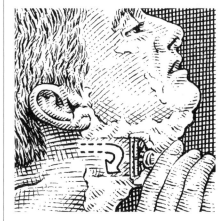

5: THE FINISHING TOUCH: "BLADE BUFFING"

Still have stubble patches? Re-lather for "blade buffing," where you scrub the razor rapidly back and forth, using short, light strokes. Note: this is the technique for a cartridge razor. "Vary the location subtly as you buff for better results." Caveat: don't try for the first time before a job interview.

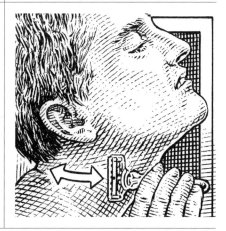

DODGE THE WATCH DIAL CON

» When Danny Pizzigoni was growing up, he developed a precocious expertise in watches. His father was in the business, and he would often accompany him to London's markets or auction houses, picking up a wealth of knowledge through osmosis. By the time Pizzigoni was 15, he knew that he could leave school and make decent money in the trade; so, at 17, that's exactly what he did.

His tactic was to buy timepieces relatively inexpensively in the UK, where demand was comparatively low, and sell them for much higher prices on the Continent. "I started developing private clients in Italy, professionals like doctors and business people, who were looking for the exceptional Patek Philippe or the very rare Rolex." Finding himself in the upper echelons of the market, in 1996 he decided to open a shop in Mayfair that was more luxurious than the competition: "It was an upmarket Bond Street shop selling upmarket Bond Street watches."

Today, it trades as The Watch Club, selling thousands of fine timepieces every year to customers from Hong Kong to America, Russia to France. It has welcomed the likes of Paul McCartney, James Corden, Arnold Schwarzenegger and Daniel Day-Lewis through its doors. Pizzigoni's popularity is partly down to his reputation: if you buy from him, you can be confident the watch authentic. "Authentic" doesn't simply mean "not fake." It also means that the dial hasn't been tampered with. If you're buying a vintage watch, it's important to make sure that the dial hasn't been restored (or "redialled," in the jargon) as this can diminish value. Here, Pizzigoni explains what to look for...

1: MAKE SURE THE DIAL SEEMS AS OLD AS THE CASE

The dial on a vintage watch ought to exhibit signs of age. For instance, white dials usually develop an opal patina over time. Also examine the "lume" — the parts of the dial that glow. "Back in the Fifties, they used radium as lume but it was very radioactive," says Pizzigoni. "A radium dial will have radium burns." Old lume should also appear dry and discolored.

2: THE DEVIL'S IN THE DETAIL

Most watch dials are printed, but restored dials are often done by hand. Look for errors, smudging and typeface inconsistencies. "Many vintage dials have beautiful serifs on even the smallest letters, and you can only see these under strong magnification. The restored dials don't have the same quality."

3: EXAMINE COMPLICATED AREAS

Places where sub-dials intersect with the main dial can look messy on a refurbished timepiece. "It's general sloppiness. Manufacturers have printing plates, laboratory conditions, and if it's not perfect, it's just scrapped and they start again. It's very difficult to replicate and get it right."

❯❯ 4: DON'T PASS THE BATON

Are there paint flecks on the hour-marker batons? Major giveaway. And if a restorer took the batons off and reattached them after working on the dial, this can also provide clues. An obvious sign would be batons not lying flat: "That means they've forced them off and they've forced them back on again."

5: COMPASS POINTS

Check whether there is a notch cut into the edge of the dial, typically at three o'clock. Restorers of early watches, who were about to take all the paint off a dial, would sometimes add this nick as a reference point to guide their repainting. This let them ensure all the new marks were correctly positioned for when the dial was fastened back to the watch. "Otherwise all of a sudden you could realize it was upside down!"

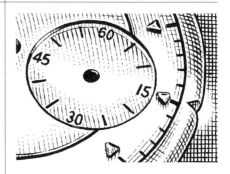

TIE A FIRST-CLASS BOW TIE

» Style rubes assume that the advantage of a "real" bow tie comes only at the end of the night, when you can unleash it and let it hang from your collar insouciantly. And, yes, that does look great. But it can be a signifier of sophistication from the get-go if others spot that you tied it yourself. So, here's a foolproof method that will not only help you succeed in knotting it (have faith), but will also give your bow a dishevelled sprezzatura. Never be mistaken for a member of the clip-on club again...

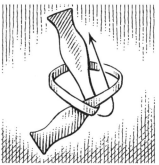

1: DRAPE AROUND YOUR NECK

Keep one end slightly longer than the other. Cross long end over short and tie a half-knot.

2: GIVE IT A TWIST

Form the short end into a bow shape. Let the other end hang over the center. Twist it once.

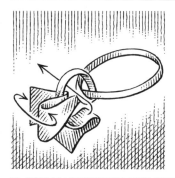

3: PINCH THE BOW TOGETHER

Form the second bow shape and push it through the hole behind the first.

4: FINESSE

Tighten and adjust, fanning the bow for just the right amount of not-giving-a-damn.

STEP UP YOUR SHOESHINE TECHNIQUE

>> Time was, every man used to know the proper way to polish his shoes. The rise of sneakers, synthetic materials and "instant shine" sponges (shudder) means that today it is becoming a forgotten art. One place where it continues to thrive, however, is George Cleverley. Founded in 1958, this London shoemaker has created footwear for everyone from Sir Michael Caine to Alexander McQueen, Jony Ive to David Beckham — and the workshop manager, Adam Law, still uses a traditional technique to achieve a gleaming shine. "The polish on the shoes also makes them more durable," says Law. "If you have a highly polished pair of shoes and you drop water on them, the water just rolls off." Here's how to look sharper for longer south of the ankle...

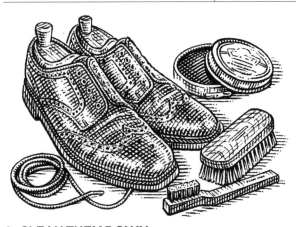

1: CLEAN THEM DOWN

Take out your laces, otherwise they'll retain polish that might rub on to your pants, and insert shoe trees so you have a solid surface on which to work. Clean the leather with a soft horsehair brush, then use a welt brush — which looks like a large toothbrush — to get into the seams. "If any dirt is left when you come to polishing the shoe, there's the potential to collect grit on your cloth or brush," says Law, "and then you might drag it all over the leather and scratch it."

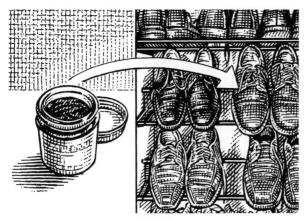

2: FEED 'EM UP (OPTIONAL)

If they are shoes that you wear regularly, proceed straight to step 3. But if they are seasonal footwear that you're about to put away in the back of your wardrobe after polishing, first apply a moisturizing leather cream with a cloth or brush. "You can be quite liberal with it — do the tongue as well — and give it time to sink in," says Law. "It's important because if the leather dries out, then it might crack and become brittle, causing it to deteriorate."

3: IT'S ALL ABOUT THAT BASE

Give your shoes a base shine. Use a round brush to apply wax polish all over the upper, the welt and into any brogue holes. "Using a brush with a smaller head is good, as it makes you work harder to get the polish into the leather." If the shoe is brown, make sure the polish is a shade lighter, but don't use "neutral" if you want to get rid of scuffs. Once you have covered the whole shoe, apply a second layer of polish, wait for 30 minutes, then buff with the horsehair brush.

4: BUST THE CLOUDS

Wrap your index finger in a lint-free cloth — Law recommends those made by Selvyt — and apply another coat of polish to the leather in circular motions about 5cm (1in) in diameter. This creates friction and helps the polish to melt. "As you're doing this, you'll see that the polish starts off looking cloudy. You want to polish all the way through that stage, keeping on with your circular motions until the polish starts to become clear." Repeat this step before moving on.

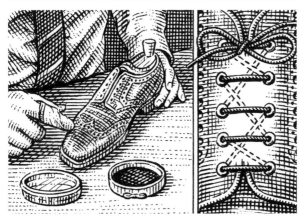

5: BUILD UP THE LAYERS

Pour some water into the lid of the polish tin. Wrap your finger in the same area of Selvyt used for applying the polish, and dip it in. Work this in circular motions over all the leather. Next, add a whole new layer of polish in circular motions, working through the cloudiness as per step 4. Then apply water again. Repeat this pattern of a layer of polish followed by water four more times. "Each time you add a layer, make the pressure slightly lighter." You should now have an extremely high shine. Lace up your shoes as shown. Step out with pride.

FASTEN A NATO WATCH STRAP

>> The simplest way to freshen up your watch is to switch its standard strap for a high-quality nylon wristband. These are not only more comfortable in warmer months but also look eminently chic. Exhibit A: James Bond's Rolex in *Goldfinger* (1964). The best type of fabric strap is a NATO. These come with an unconventional fastening that ensures the watch stays on the wrist even if one of the spring bars breaks. Created in 1973 for official military use (the name comes from its having a "NATO Stock Number"), it has become a classic the world over. Here's how to deploy it...

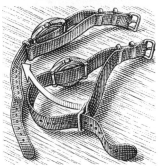

1: NAIL THE BASICS
Check the timepiece is attached to the strap properly, as depicted.

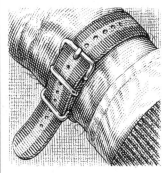

2: FASTEN AS USUAL
Stop once you reach the stage shown. You now have two options...

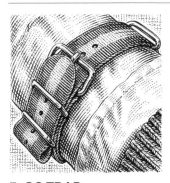

3: GO TRAD...
Fold the strap back against itself. This is the classic "quick-release" method.

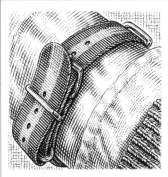

4: ...OR GO SECURE
If length permits, take the strap over the top of the furthest ring – and under the nearest.

4:

GAMES & WELL-BEING

In sport, it's often the little things that give you an edge. Small adjustments to the way you run or swim can help you go further and faster with less effort. A tweak to your squash serve can let you dominate a whole rally. Shifting the grip on your bowling ball can up your strike rate. This chapter covers all that and more, including casino games, which require an edge of a different sort. If you thought that blackjack or sports-betting were fundamentally about luck, take heed of the advice herein...

RUN LIKE AN ELITE ATHLETE

>> Running isn't taught as a skill. Unlike tennis, say, it's mostly picked up intuitively as a kind of advanced walking — and that's a problem. "We tend to run how we feel comfortable," says Mike Antoniades. "That's what makes people slow and gets them injured." A Cypriot-born former soccer player and sprinter, Antoniades has coached performance and conditioning for more than 30 years. In 2007, he set up The Running School to bring his ideas to the world.

The school now operates across six countries, and has worked with everyone from Olympic gold-medal sprinters, such as Christine Ohuruogu, to Premier League soccer players. "Some of them," says Antoniades, "come without the club knowing." Everybody requires fine-tuning specific to their own running styles but, he says, there are five principles that everyone should adopt...

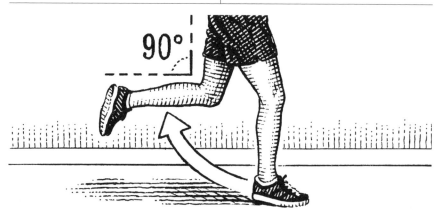

1: DON'T OVERSTEP THE MARK

Shift your center of gravity so that your foot lands underneath your hip. "When the foot goes too far forward, you brake, you start collapsing and you repeat the process," explains Antoniades. The easiest fix is to lift your heels 90 degrees behind you. This creates a cyclical motion, engaging the powerful glute and hamstring muscles to propel you forwards. Also, try landing on the ball of the foot — unless you have especially large feet, which can make this difficult.

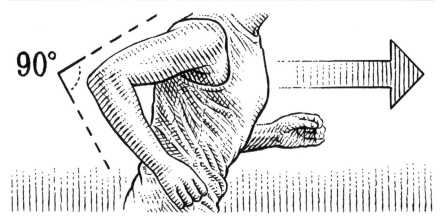

2: MORE POWER TO YOUR ELBOWS

As your elbows swing back, maintain a right-angle in the joint. This prevents rotation at the shoulders. "I call people who rotate at the shoulders 'twisters.' It makes their arms tend to come across the midline, and the counter movements put a lot of stress on different parts of their body." Although your chest will inevitably move a little, you should aim to keep it relatively flat throughout. "Not doing this is the most common problem that even elite people have."

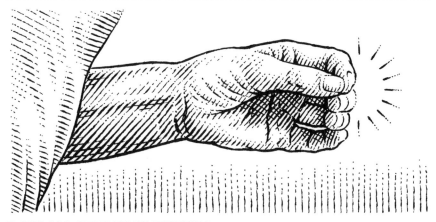

3: IT'S ALL AT YOUR FINGERTIPS

Imagine you're holding a butterfly between your thumb and index finger but not squeezing. "That relaxes the whole shoulder girdle, so you can get the elbow back easily without lifting and tightening the shoulders. The body needs rhythm and will get it any way it can. So if it doesn't get rhythm readily from the arms, it will start getting rhythm from the head — you see a lot of people running and bouncing their head — or from the mid-section." Not good.

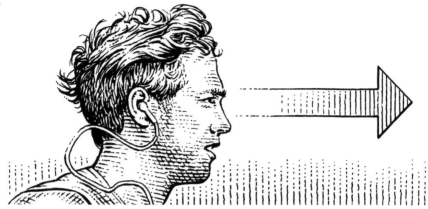

4: TALKING OF THE HEAD...

Keep an upright posture and look forward rather than down. But what if you're running on uneven terrain? "Your peripheral vision is actually quite strong. You should be able to glance down and see the ground but also be able to see ahead of you. If you look at experienced fell runners, they don't look down. They look ahead, their peripheral vision allows them to see where the foot's going to land and to make changes if they need."

5: FINALLY, PRESS PLAY

Don't run holding a music player, as it interrupts good body movement. But it is useful to carry one on your belt: Antoniades says that listening to music can boost performance by around 20 percent. Well, up to a certain level. "Elite athletes don't use music when they're going on a long run, as they want to focus. If you look at Mo Farah, he uses music only before and after as a relaxation process."

UPGRADE YOUR WORKOUT ROUTINE

» The easy part of working out is not getting injured. A little experience and a good dialogue with your body is usually enough to keep the physio away. What's harder is working out effectively. Walk into a weight room and you'll typically spy even the most fitspo gym bros fluffing it — either opting for inefficient exercises or making errors that work unintended muscles. In the long term, that can cause problems. As renowned personal trainer Jonathan Goodair puts it, "Whatever you do to your body, that's how it's going to look." Goodair has trained the likes of Madonna, Cate Blanchett, Ralph Fiennes, rugby internationals and a host of others for whom getting the wrong body is not an option. So, next time you hit the gym, here's how to perfect five simple exercises you're probably getting wrong.

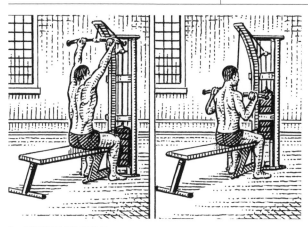

1: BICEP CURLS

The mistake: Doing bicep curls.

Do underhand-grip pull-downs instead. These work the biceps and much more. Sit comfortably with a straight posture. Grab the bar but don't raise your shoulders — keep the shoulder blades down and the collarbones wide. As you draw the bar down to the top of your chest, allow your elbows to move slightly backward. When you release the bar, do so slowly, allowing your arms to reach full extension, without elevating your shoulders, before pulling it back again. Crucially, never pull it down behind your neck.

2: BENT-OVER BARBELL ROW

The mistake: An overhand grip.

"I do an underhand grip, so I work the lats, middle back muscles, and the biceps, too." Combining all those muscles in one exercise can save you at least 15 minutes in the gym. The other things to avoid are letting your arms hang from their joints, rather than holding the shoulders stable, and pulling the bar up into your chest. "We don't want all the focus on that upper-back area, we want to keep that wide as we work. So, instead, bring the bar into your stomach."

3: ABDOMINAL CRUNCHES

The mistake: Sitting up fully.

"A lot of people do abdominal crunches, and a lot of people do them wrong." If you sit up all the way, your abs only work through half of their range, then your hip flexors kick in to bring you upright. An ideal crunch, instead, isolates the abdominals. "Put your hands behind your head, supporting the weight of your head — chin down slightly, elbows just in your peripheral vision." Drop your shoulders away from your ears. Inhale to prepare and, as you exhale, curl forward, looking toward your belly button, then slowly come back down.

4: BARBELL SQUATS

The mistake: Leaning forward.

If you put your shoulders and head forward, you're lifting with your lower back. "That's very, very typical of so many people." The correct form is as shown. Push your hips backward to go into the squat. "Ideally, get down to a position where your thighs are pretty much parallel with the floor but you're maintaining the same neutral shape in your back." Your thighs and feet should be aligned and your knees shouldn't come forward any farther than your toes.

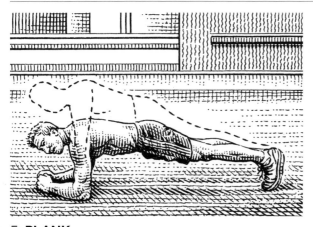

5: PLANK

The mistake: The wrong goals.

"Some people will say the correct plank position is when your ears, shoulders, hips and heels are at the same height. But I think you'd need quite big feet for that, somehow. For me, I focus more on the ears, shoulders and hips being aligned." Once you've refined the position, you could just hold it — but that's quite tedious. Instead, try changing up the exercise with moves such as toe taps or moving from a plank to push-up position and back again (see picture). "I would do a whole sequence of variations that takes about six minutes." Now that's a workout.

HIT AN EVIL SQUASH SERVE

>> When serving in squash, it's rare to hit an outright winner. That can lead players to neglect the importance of the shot, viewing it simply as a way of starting a rally. But be under no illusions, says Nick Matthew, "the serve is crucial". Matthew is one of the greatest squash players that Britain has ever produced. He is the first Englishman to have won the British Open three times, and one of only six players on the planet to have won the World Championship three times. To him, serving is the best opportunity you have to gain an edge.

"It's the only time you have control of the pace of the game, it's the only time you reset and center your mindset — and you can set yourself up for being on the 'T.'" The "T," of course, is where the lines intersect at the center of the court; whoever stands there tends to dominate the point. "So you want to push your opponent back with the serve — make sure they have a difficult return, make sure they can't attack the ball — and set a platform for the rest of the rally." It helps to surprise your rival with different types of serve: there's the smash serve, for instance, where the ball is thumped just above the service line; or the body serve, which bounces directly at your opponent. The nuclear option, however, is the lob. "It is the hardest serve to return," says Matthew, "but it is the riskiest to play." Here's how to do it, based on a right-hander serving from the right-hand side...

1: TAKE A STANCE

Stand with your back foot in the service box, your weight on that leg and your body at 45 degrees to the side wall. "Make sure the grip is light," says Matthew. "The fingers need to be able to work the racket for accuracy — just as darts players throw from their fingers rather than their palm."

2: IT'S A TOSS-UP

You're going to hit underarm with an open racket face, so you need to toss the ball accordingly. "You want to get under the ball; you're not going to toss it much higher than chest height."

3: WORK THE ANGLES

Aim about half a racket's length below the top "out-of-court" line, such that the ball bounces high on the left side wall. "Follow the line of the ball with your follow-through, very much like a golf swing. That will not only help your accuracy but it will propel the momentum of your body weight to the 'T.'"

›› 4: PACE IT

The strike should be just powerful enough that the ball comes off the front and side walls like a dead weight, making your opponent uncertain about whether to volley. Ideally, it should then bounce on the floor just before hitting the back wall. "Then they're playing a defensive shot from the go."

5: "T" TIME

Immediately after serving, move quickly to the "T." At this point, you may be tempted to look toward the front wall. That's a mistake. "Your head should be turned, never taking your eye off the ball for a split second." That way you can respond instantly to the return. If it comes.

SWIM FASTER, EASIER FRONT CRAWL

>> When Steven Shaw was 17, he made a tough decision. Throughout his teenage years, he had been an obsessive swimmer, competing at county level, but he had begun to find the sport frustrating. "Swimming left me feeling burned-out and tired," recalls the Londoner. "I couldn't really understand why my performance wasn't improving even though I was training really hard." Having developed back and neck issues, he decided to give it up altogether.

At university, however, he chanced upon the Alexander Technique. Developed by the Australian actor Frederick Matthias Alexander in the 1890s, it teaches improved movement and posture in daily life. Shaw became fascinated by its implications for sport. "If you can improve the relationship between your head, neck and back," he says, "your performance in any activity will get much better." He wondered if it could help him rediscover swimming. There was not much research on using the technique in the water, so he broke down each stroke into its smallest constituent parts, examined their effect on his back, and endeavored to refine the movements. As he progressed, the results were transformative. "My performance got better," he recalls, "but the amount of fatigue significantly reduced." And so the Shaw Method was born.

Today, Shaw's swimming technique has been taught to thousands of people across the globe, from Greece to America, Britain to Japan. His company, Art of Swimming, counts among its clients professional swimmers — both current Olympians and former greats — as well as politicians and celebrities. The impact he has had on their stroke has afforded him a kind of cult status. We asked him to explain five steps to faster, easier front crawl...

» 1: DON'T WINDMILL

Only start pulling back with one hand as the other enters the water (fingertips first, with your thumb pointing down). That's because if you were to pull back while your other hand was still behind you, says Shaw, "you wouldn't be able to put all of your body weight on to the pulling arm."

2: EFFICIENCY IS EVERYTHING

When pulling backward, use the whole of your lower arm as a paddle. As you do so, stretch the front "directional arm" forward (this is your rudder) and rotate the hand into a "handshake" position. "This opens up the hip on the other side, turning it up toward the ceiling." Allow your body — but not your head — to rotate with it, thus reducing drag.

3: NAIL THE BREATHING

On the first arm cycle, look straight down, holding your breath; on the second, look slightly forward and slowly exhale; on the third, rotate your head with your body and calmly inhale. "Rather than 'taking a breath,' *allow* the air to come in. It's almost like the movement is breathing you."

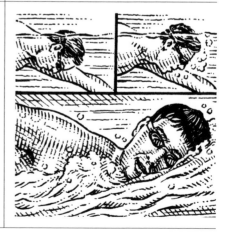

4: DIG DEEP

Keep the front, directional arm pointing downward. This will help raise your rear arm as it flies out of the water, affording you more time to breathe. To save energy, keep that rear arm loose as it comes forward again and re-enters the water. "That's a non-propulsive movement; if you put effort into that movement, it creates counter propulsion."

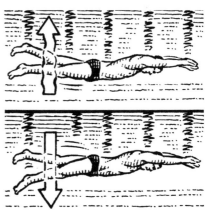

5: FOR KICKS

Kick from your hips, only putting effort into the downward movement and allowing your legs to float back up. Aim for two kicks for every arm cycle. "The front-crawl kick is primarily there for balance, rhythm and stability. The mistake people make is kicking too fast — that will wear you out." It all comes down to this: relax.

POWER-THROW A FOOTBALL

>> Even if you don't follow football or have never played it, there may come a time when you are required to chuck a football around at a barbecue. It would be churlish not to join in — and if you are going to take part, you ought to be able to throw a decent pass. "The ball is built to spiral so the receiver can catch it a lot easier," says Emmanuel Sanders, who won the Super Bowl in 2016 with the NFL's Denver Broncos. Here's how you give the ball that crucial spin...

1: TAKE HOLD OF THE LACES

Grip the back of the ball. Generally speaking, your ring and little fingers should rest against the ball's laces. "If you can't find the laces, your chances of throwing a spiral go down," says Sanders. The thumb should make an "L" shape with your index finger, which, in turn, should lie across the seam.

2: COCK THE ARM

Stand at 90 degrees to your target and bring the ball up to head height, using the other hand to steady it. Pull your arm back in preparation for the throw, your elbow behind you and a right-angle between your upper arm and forearm.

3: FIND YOUR FEET

Rather than rooting your feet to the ground, keep them moving and stay light on your toes. Initially, hold your weight on your back leg, then step into the pass with your forward foot for extra momentum as you throw.

4: RELEASE THE MISSILE

Project your arm powerfully forward, squaring up your body at the target and releasing the ball at the highest point of the arc. Follow through, allowing your back leg to come forward and your hand to come to rest by your opposite leg.

5: GIVE IT A SPIN

"The moment you release that football, you want to see it spinning off the tips of your fingers." It should come off your index finger last. Physicists will tell you that spinning the ball gives it "angular momentum," ensuring a longer, more accurate pass.

FREEDIVE LIKE A MERMAN

» Some say that humans were born to dive. Like aquatic mammals, we exhibit a "diving reflex": when immersed, the body redistributes its blood supply to the vital organs, the heart rate slows down and the spleen contracts to expel oxygen-rich blood cells. What's more, our species has been exploring the depths for millennia. Plato, for instance, writes about Ancient Greeks washing with natural sponges that would have been picked from around 30m (100ft) below the surface. But it wasn't until the 20th century, thanks to the invention of masks and flippers, that freediving — diving without breathing apparatus — took off as a recreational activity. Herbert Nitsch is one of its masters. The "deepest man on earth," he holds the sport's record for a descent of 253m (830ft) — and he is the only freediver with world records across all of its eight disciplines.

To him, the appeal goes well beyond competition. "I used to scuba dive in the beginning, but I found I'd much rather freedive," he says. The main reason was that it allowed him to see a greater abundance of marine life. "With scuba diving you only see creatures that are not afraid of noise — the bubbles from breathing are extremely loud. Also, with freediving, you can move much more easily in all directions, which is something that we land creatures are not used to." So what makes him a better freediver than the next guy? "The main thing is mental, but the physical aspect is also important. It's about understanding how your body works and influencing it in the best way."

Here's Nitsch's advice for beginners. Freediving is inherently dangerous, so only ever try this at your own risk and with the approval and supervision of a professional instructor...

1: PRACTICE YOUR BREATH HOLDS ON LAND

Relax, exhale everything and don't breathe for, say, 30 seconds. Breathe normally for the same period then repeat, but for slightly longer. Continue repeating the cycle for about an hour. "If you do this daily for seven days prior to a freediving holiday, you can expect to double your breath-hold."

100%→200%

2: KEEP YOURSELF IN GOOD SHAPE

It's essential to keep the diaphragm and lungs flexible, in order to improve maximum and minimum lung volume. A good training tool is to breathe out and use your chest muscles to pull your diaphragm up and down multiple times. When the urge to breathe arises, take a sip of air and continue until you have to breathe fully.

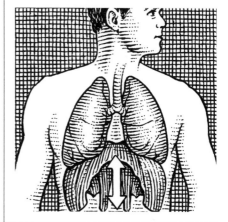

3: BUDDY UP

Never dive alone. Most blackouts happen at the surface, and those who dive deeper than 60m (197ft) risk nitrogen narcosis, which has a similar effect to being drunk. "To get used to this, I recommend 'narcosis training' on land. This exercise consists of getting well liquored up and attempting practical tasks."

➤➤ 4: BREATHE UP TO GO DOWN

Nitsch takes deep, long "breathe-ups" for five to ten minutes prior to diving, which causes hyperventilation. "Most freedivers think that hyperventilation is a no-go, but I strongly believe it is necessary." The urge to breathe is due to carbon dioxide. Hyperventilation lowers CO_2 levels, which extends your time below the surface.

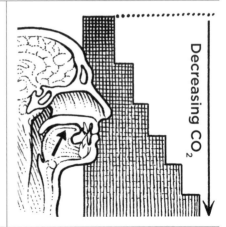

Decreasing CO_2

5: TIME TO EXPLORE

While diving, get speed by scissor-kicking with bi-fins from your hips and knees. "To maximize a freedive depth or duration, you need to minimize oxygen consumption by keeping mentally calm and by physically moving as little as possible — otherwise, adrenaline rushes through your veins and your heart rate rises." Just relax.

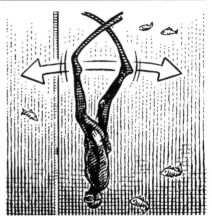

WIN BIG AT THE CASINO

>> The old Wilson Mizner quip has it that gambling is "the sure way of getting nothing for something." Yet mathematicians have long attempted to flip that idea on its head and topple Lady Luck from her pedestal — with a surprising degree of success. Some of their techniques are grounded in traditional problem-solving, but others have been gleaned through new breakthroughs in machine-learning and artificial intelligence. In the process, games that seemed impossible to model have revealed themselves to be laden with patterns. Take football. "Despite the messy, complicated series of individual interactions that drives this game, we can still develop enough understanding to make decent predictions," says Adam Kucharski, whose book *The Perfect Bet* (2016) offers a lucid survey of how smart gamblers are giving the house a run for its money. We asked for his advice on five games...

1: PLAY HEADS-UP LIMIT HOLD-'EM POKER LIKE A BOT

In 2015, the University of Alberta unveiled a computer program called Cepheus, which is unbeatable in heads-up limit hold-'em. We can learn from how it plays. Its behavior confirms that the dealer has the advantage and that you should raise or fold on your first go, rather than "limping." Contrary to received wisdom, however, supposedly useless hands (offsuit four and six, say) are occasionally worth playing, and even with a pair of aces it is rarely advisable to bet the maximum stake. "In poker your aim is to make your opponent's decisions as difficult as possible," observes Kucharski.

2: CARD-COUNTING ISN'T THE ONLY BLACKJACK STRATEGY

Not enough people make their decision based on the dealer's upturned card — but they should. That's because casino rules typically dictate that dealers must keep drawing cards until their total is greater than 16. There are more cards in the deck worth ten than any other. "So, if the dealer is showing a very low face-up card, because of the rules they have to follow, there's quite a high chance that they have to draw too many cards and go bust. Even when you've got a 12 or 13 — if the dealer's showing a five, stick."

3: EMBRACE SOCCER'S GOLDEN MINUTE

Analysts have found clear patterns in soccer. In general, the betting marketplace overreacts to dramatic events, and this creates a window of uncertainty that usually lasts around a minute. You can exploit this by finding odds that underprice the likely outcome. There's a misconception, for instance, that teams are vulnerable after scoring a goal — stats show that's not true, and nor are red cards as devastating as imagined. "In reality the team can adjust." In terms of betting on a specific outcome, here's a tip: if the score line is 0–0 after 80 minutes, a draw becomes much more likely.

4: TENNIS IS RIPE FOR ARBITRAGE

Pros understand arbitrage, but beginners may not. "Arbitrage is when there's something on offer for two different prices in two different places. You buy it at the cheaper place and sell it to the more expensive place." So, with a tennis match, you may be able to use the internet to find two bookmakers each offering a good price on the other player. Whoever wins, the bookmaker with whom you had good odds for that player will give you a payout that subsidizes your loss with the other and vice versa.

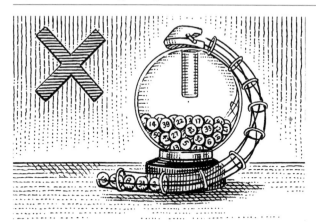

5: NEVER PLAY LOTTERIES

There's a formula called the Kelly Criterion that tells you how much money you should bet on a particular game. It argues that you should only risk a specific percentage of your bankroll, calculated by dividing expected payoff by maximum potential winnings. For lotteries, the Kelly Criterion suggests that it's only worth playing if you have a huge bankroll. "If you have ten billion dollars, and the Powerball rolled over for a few weeks, even then the Kelly Criterion would be telling you only to buy a few dozen tickets." In other words, you may as well not bother.

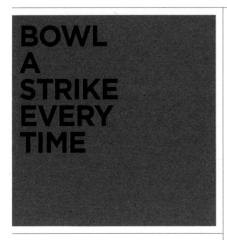

BOWL A STRIKE EVERY TIME

>> It's easy to be good at bowling but it's difficult to be great. "A typical amateur might just throw the ball down there and probably one out of ten times they're going to get a strike," says Walter Ray Williams Jr. "A professional probably averages about 60 percent strikes, maybe 70." Williams speaks from experience. The Californian-born pro has been anointed Player of the Year by the Professional Bowlers Association (PBA) seven times since beginning his career in 1980, and he holds the record for PBA Tour all-time titles. His nickname? Deadeye, for his precision.

Williams's first piece of advice is to pick the correct weight of ball. Plenty of amateurs believe that they should veer toward heavy. Actually, a lighter ball can help with spin. Got your rock? Here's how to throw it...

1: KNUCKLE DOWN

Sink your middle finger, ring finger and thumb inside the ball. The thumb should go all the way in, but it's up to you what you do with the fingers. "Typically a beginner bowler's going to put their fingers down to the second knuckle from the tip — that would be the conventional grip," says Williams. "But the fingertip grip — only inserting to the first knuckle from the tip — allows your fingers to put more rotation on the ball. Typically most of the pros are going to put their fingers just in to the fingertips."

2: POCKET IT

See those arrows a short way up the lane? They're to help you aim. Bowling alleys coat their lanes in oil and, under typical conditions, where the oil is distributed evenly, you want to throw the ball along the above trajectory. The aim is to hit the "pocket" between the pin at the front of the triangle, and the one diagonally backward from it to the right. Left-handers should aim for the pocket on the other side (and should flip right for left in all subsequent instructions).

3: VISUALIZE YOUR APPROACH

Plan a four-step run-up to the foul line. You'll see a row of dots just behind it to help you judge your positioning. If a lane has been evenly oiled, you should bowl from the first dot to the right of the center. As ball after ball is flung down toward the pins, however, the oil pattern will change, and you will notice the balls behaving differently. Adjust your positioning to compensate.

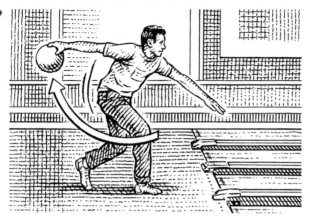

4: SWING!

For the first step of your four-step delivery, start on your right foot and extend the ball outward toward the pins before letting it swing down. On the second step, the ball should be swinging back past your legs. On the third step, the ball should be at the top of your backswing. As it comes down, embrace its pendulum motion. "Let the ball determine your arm swing and don't fight it." Then slide into the final step, at which point "you want to get a good knee bend, with the toe, knee and chin in a straight line."

5: ROLL WITH IT

Release the ball at the bottom of your downward swing, by your ankle, letting your thumb come out first. "As you let go with the fingers, they are going to lift and put rotation on the ball." This counterclockwise motion should come from the wrist, not the arm, and then you should follow through. Watch the pins tumble; celebratory Big Lebowski references optional.

DE-STRESS WITH MINDFUL MEDITATION

>> Mindful meditation may have its roots in Buddhism, but its effects are not a matter of faith. Scientific studies using MRI scans have shown that practitioners' brains recalibrate to deal better with stress, for instance, and anxiety. So what exactly is mindfulness? Jon Kabat-Zinn, who is widely credited with popularizing it in the West, defines it thus: "The awareness that arises from paying attention on purpose in the present moment, non-judgmentally." He has been advocating this kind of "awareness" since founding the Mindfulness-Based Stress Reduction (MBSR) program at the University of Massachusetts back in 1979. Over the following decades, Kabat-Zinn's theories slowly went mainstream. "All of a sudden it's on everybody's lips," he says. "The reason for that is that the science of mindfulness has really grown exponentially." Here's his beginner's guide...

1: TAKE YOURSELF OFF

Put on relaxing clothes and find a calm spot away from interruptions. "The most important thing is to find somewhere you feel at home. It could be a favorite chair — though a straight-back chair is better than falling into a plush couch or armchair — or a meditation cushion on the floor." Decide how long you wish to meditate for; 15 minutes is a good place to start. "You can set timers, but if it goes tick-tock, it will drive you crazy," he says. "I just put my watch in front of me and look at that."

2: SITTING COMFORTABLY?

If you're sitting on a chair, place both feet on the floor; if you're on the floor, use a cushion, but make sure it's stable. As for posture: "It's important to sit in a posture that embodies dignity and wakefulness, whatever that means to the person.

As soon as you do that, it's very reassuring. It says, 'You are dignified — you already have that,' so operationalize that in your spine."

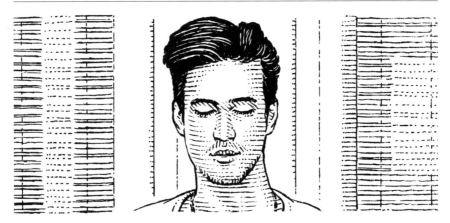

3: DE-FRAZZLE

Shut your eyes or focus in the mid-distance. Allow your mind to calm, which can be easier said than done. "The best advice that I know is to assume that your mind will settle all by itself. If you take a bottle of apple juice, the kind with pulp in it, and shake it up, it'll be cloudy. But if you put it on a shelf,

it will eventually clear." And if your mind doesn't settle? "Don't fight it. If you have an unpleasant thought, just notice that 'that's an unpleasant thought.' The importance is the awareness of that, as awareness is exactly what mindfulness is cultivating."

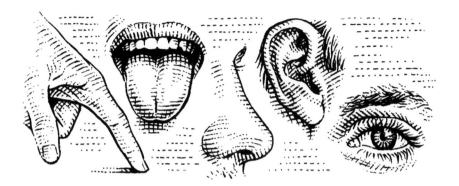

4: GET MINDFUL

Become hyper-aware of all five senses. Notice what it feels like to inhabit your body, all the way to your fingers and toes. Notice your breath flowing in and out, notice even the pauses between breaths. "When you're beginning, the mind tends to be very agitated — one moment you're in awareness, the next moment you're having some kind of fantasy and ten minutes later you realize you were supposed to be meditating. It is very helpful to stabilize your awareness by focussing on one thing — your breath."

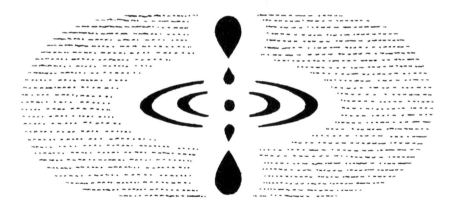

5: STAY, DON'T STRAY

If your thoughts wander, don't worry. This is guaranteed to happen. "Every time, what you do is notice what's on your mind — perhaps you're imagining a fight you're going to have with your boss — and then you just bring your thoughts back to your belly and to your breathing. You do that a million times if necessary, and don't give yourself a hard time about it."

5:

ON THE MOVE

A few years ago, *GQ*'s deputy editor Bill Prince showed me how to fold a suit so that it didn't crease in my suitcase. Having learned the required origami, I found myself using it so often that I ended up junking my suit carrier altogether. You'll find the method in this chapter alongside a wealth of advice from external experts, plus an array of other travel hacks long-valued by the editors at *GQ*. The tips for sleeping on a night flight or upgrading your hotel experience, for instance, have been passed through generations of staffers — and now to you...

OPTIMIZE YOUR HOTEL EXPERIENCE

» Keep this in mind: while the hotel is ostensibly there to serve you, it's really there to serve itself. If the staff think they can get away with providing the bare minimum, even if the bare minimum is nonetheless extremely luxurious, or adding a charge to your bill — no matter how overpriced — they won't bat an eyelid. Nothing personal, just business. So you need to approach your stay like booking a flight: aim to get the very best for your money, and stay wise to the industry's ploys...

1: LOYALTY GOES A LONG WAY

Hotels care about repeat business, so you'll get treated better if you opt for a place that knows you. Join the loyalty program, obviously, and make sure you book directly — not least because guests for whom the hotel does not have to pay a third-party commission are looked upon favorably.

2: BOOK THE ROOM, NOT THE HOTEL

If you're hoping for an upgrade, book at least a middle-tier room and make sure you know its full specs and location within the building. Haggle over the price — there will always be special rates available, particularly if you're a regular, a business traveller or staying for any length of time.

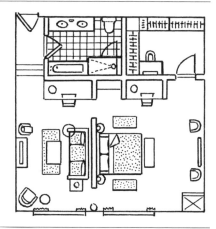

3: USE CHECK-IN TO SET THE TONE

If you're working, tell the check-in desk you're going to be using the hotel as a base, hosting meetings and dinners. They will take care of you as you're bringing in business. Similarly, if it's a special occasion, make them aware. Finally, turn on the charm and request an upgrade. You may have greater success with that if checking in later in the day.

4: SEE THE ROOM BEFORE YOU UNPACK

Make sure it's exactly what you expected. If it's by the elevator or above the restaurant, ask them to do better. Even if you only have a small niggle, it's worth voicing it: the hotel might offer you a gift such as a spa treatment by way of compensation.

5: DON'T BE AN IN-ROOM ROOKIE

There are two things that will rack up charges beyond all reasonable expectations: the phone and the minibar. This new era of cheap mobile-phone roaming charges means you should never use the former, and the local convenience store means you should never use the latter — especially for bottled water.

TRACK STAND LIKE A CHAMPION CYCLIST

» Balancing on a bike while it's not moving (a "track stand") is famously difficult. "I've been riding a bike since I was five years old, and I still struggle with it sometimes," says Chris Akrigg. "If I can pull off a perfect track stand at a set of traffic lights, I feel good about it."

That's saying something coming from him. The Yorkshireman is one of the greatest trials riders in the world and has won the British Trials Championship on six occasions. It's his astonishing bike-handling skills, however, that have won him an audience well beyond cycling nuts. Online videos of Akrigg riding daring lines and pulling stunts have been watched by millions.

Track standing is vital to what Akrigg does. "If you're doing any sort of skill on the bike, everything starts from a track stand. And certainly, if you're trying to tackle obstacles, it's all about slowing down, balancing and sizing up what's ahead of you." That said, the technique itself was born worlds away from the great outdoors, on the boards of the velodrome. Riders would use it to balance on the pedals behind the start line, so as soon as the start gun fired, they could be off. Subsequently it was adopted by road cyclists, because it let them hold themselves at a standstill – at traffic lights, say – without unclipping their shoes from the pedals.

It's easiest to do on a fixed gear bike, where pedalling backwards moves the bike backwards – this helps centre your balance. On a standard bike (one with gears), you don't have the option of backpedalling, which makes it considerably trickier. This is for a bike with gears...

1: FIND YOUR LEVEL

Shift into a middle gear and slow to almost stationary. Centre your balance and get your feet into position. "Your crank arms should be level," says Akrigg. "You want your best foot forward – that's the one you'd have in front if you were freewheeling down a hill."

2: GIVE IT A BRAKE

Lift yourself off the saddle, moving your weight slightly forwards. Put a fair amount of weight on your handlebars and through the front of the bike. Feather the front brake, so if you're losing your balance, you can gently pedal against the resistance to recentre.

3: TURN INTO THE FALL

Turn your front wheel 45 degrees either left or right. This will help you prop yourself up. "Then, to keep your balance, you just make little adjustments left and right on the wheel." Twitch left if you're falling to the left and right if you're falling to the right.

⟫ 4: LEAN IN, LEAN OUT

As you improve, try to minimise the amount you need to move the wheel by leaning to one side or the other to maintain balance. An alternative is to use your leg as a counterweight. "When your feet are clipped in, you can swing your front knee in and out to stay steady."

5: WHAT IF YOU EDGE TOO FAR FORWARD?

It's best to track stand against a slight incline (try turning your wheel up into the camber of the road) so you can roll backwards. If that's not possible – and you've moved too far – lock the front brake and throw your weight forwards, raising your back wheel. As it falls, release the brake and you'll roll back.

START A FIRE IN THE RAIN

» Charles Darwin considered humanity's mastery of fire to be its greatest achievement after language. Our ability to create and sustain a flame stretches back hundreds of thousands of years. And yet, today, it's becoming a marginalized skill. That's unfortunate, because being able to start a fire might just save your life if you're stranded while out trekking. Jason Ingamells, an award-winning bushcraft expert who has worked widely in Africa and the Arctic, laments how "having a connection back to the natural world is something that's so dramatically lacking both in adults' and children's lives." Hence his UK-based company Woodland Ways, which offers instruction on outdoor survival. Fire-building is the linchpin of much of what he teaches...

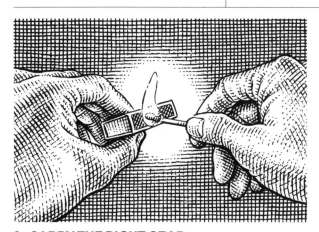

1: CARRY THE RIGHT GEAR

You could hope to start your fire by rubbing sticks together or striking stones, but that's tricky and, if you're a beginner, unreliable. "Why would you do that if you can carry something with you that would give you that heat source in the first place?" says Ingamells. Aside from obvious heat sources, such as matches or a lighter, you could also consider carrying a firesteel or a ferrocerium rod. The latter creates sparks of up to 3,000°C (5,430°F) and is not only durable but also works in high winds.

2: COLLECT THREE TYPES OF WOOD

The first thing you want to collect is tinder. This is material that will ignite in a few seconds and get the fire going. Birch bark works well, as do fine shavings from larger pieces of wood. The second type of wood you need is kindling — smaller pieces of wood to ignite the larger pieces — varying from the width of a matchstick to the width of your little finger. The final ingredient is your main pieces of fuel. Collect as much as possible before it rains, but if it's wet already...

3: PREPARE THE WOOD

For fuel and kindling, select pieces that don't feel soft when you press them with your thumb. You will need to split the fuel to expose the dry material. Place a knife across its diameter. Strike the back of the knife repeatedly with another piece of wood. "The shock waves split it straight down through the weak point." Keep splitting it until it is just bigger than your wrist. Check that the wood really is dry by placing it against your lower lip and seeing if it pulls at the skin when you lift it away (wet wood won't).

4: BUILD THE FIRE

Head to a sheltered site. Woodland with a broadleaf or coniferous canopy would work, but scrape away all organic material nearby to reduce the risk of fire-spread, and don't cook next to a tree. Dig a depression about the size of a wok. Place some small pieces of wood across the bottom, running in the same direction. Add two handfuls of tinder, and use your heat source to get an initial flame. Now start to build a pyramid on top using kindling, beginning with matchstick-size pieces and working up to knee height.

5: ONCE THE KINDLING IS ROARING

It's now time to add fuel. If you keep creating a pyramid, "you're going to end up with a fire that's unsafe because it will collapse." Instead, carefully flatten the pyramid and lay fuel horizontally. How you do this is determined by the kind of fire you want to create. For a fast-burning, bright fire, lay the fuel in a crisscross pattern. For a slower burn, lay all the fuel in the same direction; this can also provide a stable platform to cook on. Once the fire is well-established, stash the rest of your wood on the far side to bounce the heat back at you.

FOLD A SUIT FOR CREASE-FREE TRAVEL

>> We've all been guilty of it at some point or another, but dragging your suit around in its protective zip-up cover is definitely a "don't." That's partly down to style snobbery (well, do *you* think it's a good look?) and partly to bad experiences (it's actually not a great way to keep your precious cargo free from wrinkles) — but mostly because it's a pain to carry. You could buy luggage with a dedicated suit compartment, but there's no reason why you shouldn't just pack your suit in your case with everything else. All you need is a little sartorial origami...

1: MAKE THE JACKET WORK FOR YOU

Use the jacket as a packing tool to keep pocket squares flat (load them into the breast pocket) and cufflinks safe (drop them into a side pocket) in transit. Then put one hand inside each shoulder and press your palms together, folding the shoulders back against themselves.

2: NEST THE SHOULDERS

With your right hand, grip the armhole of the other shoulder through the fabric. Remove your left hand, and use it to raise and grip the jacket's collar. Uncross your hands, pulling carefully in opposite directions to turn the jacket inside out. One shoulder will now be tucked into the other.

3: THE FINISHING MOVE

Adjust the jacket so the lapels align, and then push the shoulders back through the other way. The jacket is now precisely folded, and its structure will hold it in place. It is also inside out, so if any damage is done to your bag, the lining should take the hit. Release your left hand from the lapels and lay the jacket on your bed.

4: ROLL DON'T FOLD

Stuff the shoulder cavity with soft items, such as underwear or rolled-up T-shirts. Next, carefully roll the jacket up, starting from the shoulders. This approach will reduce the overall volume as well as minimize creases.

5: FINALLY, THE TROUSERS

Place your pants flat on the bed. Layer any other pairs of pants on top in alternating directions and — crucially — add one or two soft items such as sweaters for padding. Starting from the pant hems on the bottom layer, fold upward (two to three folds is about right) to form a neat package. Place this and the jacket in your case. You're ready to hit the road.

GET QUALITY SLEEP ON A NIGHT FLIGHT

>> Overnight flights are a necessary evil (and if you're flying economy, they're arguably just evil). No matter how much airlines invest in trying to make them more like a living-room experience and less like an enhanced interrogation, getting quality shut-eye in a stuffy, crowded cabin might seem impossible. Except: talk to someone who flies frequently, and they'll almost certainly have sleep-inducing rituals and routines that they swear by. The writers and editors here at *GQ* are an itinerant bunch, often flying around the world for stories, photoshoots and fashion shows. Here are our collective, hard-won tips...

1: UNDER PRESSURE

At the booking stage, try to fly on a plane with higher cabin pressure, such as a Boeing 787. This artificially lowers the altitude, in turn boosting oxygen levels in your bloodstream and improving your comfort. If you are flying in economy, try to book the exit row — this may come at a small premium but the extra leg room will pay dividends.

2: GET BUSY

You might have the final hours of a business trip to yourself, but don't give in to temptation and spend them by the pool. Organize a packed day prior to flying and try to tire yourself out. Before boarding, eat a light dinner so you don't have to wait for the in-flight meal service.

3: KEEP WATCH

On the plane, set your watch to the arrival time zone. This will help you work out your sleep schedule and focus your mind on the need to get some rest.

4: THE SECRET INGREDIENTS

Avoid looking at screens — the light will make you feel awake. Instead, read a book and drink two glasses of red wine (any less won't help; any more will give you a hangover). Others like to take a mild, over-the-counter sedative, though only use as directed.

5: BLOCK OUT STIMULI

Sleep mask, earplugs — they're provided for a reason. Sitting in economy? Place a travel pillow around the front of your neck for a nod-free flight (looks strange but it's worth it). Make sure your seatbelt is fastened and visible, and tell the flight attendant you don't wish to be disturbed. See you on the other side.

DRIVE LIKE A "HEEL-AND-TOE" PRO

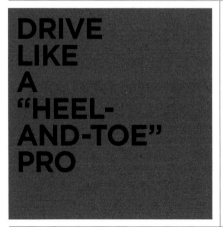

>> When performance drivers shift down a gear to take a tight corner, they often call on a trick from the golden age of motoring: heel-and-toe. "It's for when you want a seamless downchange," says Ben Collins, the former Stig on BBC's *Top Gear* and author of *How to Drive* (2014). Without heel-and-toe, you risk sudden deceleration and skidding. While the technique is only necessary for everyday driving if you're behind the wheel of a classic, such as an Aston Martin DB5, it remains useful in modern cars in bad conditions or at high speeds. "If you find yourself in a hot pursuit in the Alps, then heel-and-toe is on."

1: COME OFF THE GAS

A technique for manual cars, heel-and-toe is used to match the engine speed to that of the wheels during braking. This can be vital when you've downshifted for a corner, because on clutch release, a mismatched engine speed can cause problems. First, apply the brake.

2: GO NEUTRAL

Push down on the clutch with your left foot, move the stick out of gear— and keep braking. "Once you start braking, you ideally don't come off the brake until you turn into the corner," says Collins. Amateurs often brake multiple times — that's inefficient.

3: BLIP THE THROTTLE

While still squeezing the clutch and brake, use the brake foot to simultaneously "blip" the accelerator. "All cars are different. If the pedals are too far apart to easily overlap them with the front of your foot, keep the ball of your foot on the brake and stretch across with your heel to work the accelerator." This is the "heel-and-toe" action.

4: ENGAGE GEAR

Once the engine is up to speed, put the stick into gear and take your foot off the clutch. Note that diesel engines may take a while to respond to the blip, whereas "with a V10 monster, you just give it a snap of the throttle, the revs will fly up, and at that point you can declutch."

5: PICK UP SPEED

Get off the brake, take the corner and, as your steering straightens on the way out, drive off. Oh, and why not make like Collins and use heel-and-toe for hill starts, too? "It's a cheat really: I put my foot on the footbrake, cover the accelerator with the same foot, and pull away without using the handbrake."

SPEED-LEARN ANY LANGUAGE

>> The Foreign Service Institute is tasked with getting American diplomats fluent in foreign languages within a matter of months. One of the keys to its approach is to focus on teaching what staff actually need to know — there's no point in a diplomat memorizing arcane musical terms if they want to negotiate trade deals. "We don't teach Russian," says James Bernhardt, the FSI's Director of Curriculum, "we teach people to *use* Russian." Here, Bernhardt and his colleague Catherine Doughty, Director for Romance Languages, explain how to turbo-charge the process...

1: IMMERSE YOURSELF FULLY

"Learning by doing engages all the right brain processes and memory processes," says Doughty. Aside from the obvious — watching the news in that language, traveling to the country — try changing the language on your computer. Also, watch online videos of native speakers doing activities you plan to do.

2: GET SMART WITH VOCAB

Learning the top 1,000 most frequently used words will let you understand around 70 percent of what you encounter. Get a list weighted for your purposes (rather than simply a "general" list), but do add in well-chosen, low-frequency words. "For us," says Bernhardt, "the word for 'embassy' has got to be in the first week."

3: DON'T SWEAT THE GRAMMAR

It's ineffective to start off by rote-learning reams of grammatical rules. Much better to receive a short explanation of a point of grammar as and when you need it. So get using the language and wait for corrective feedback. This will either happen naturally or you can say to a friend: "If I keep making an error, please tell me."

4: STICK 'EM UP

It's a common memory tactic to label household objects with their foreign names using Post-it notes. However, people often make the mistake of writing the words on the front of the Post-its; actually, it's better to put them on the back, forcing you to mentally retrieve the word. If you can't remember it, then it's easy to check.

5: KNOW YOUR TRUE FRIENDS

"True friends" are words in a foreign language that are nearly identical to their equivalents in yours. "That's a good shortcut," says Doughty. "But there are also false friends. Find a list of these so you know when you hear that word it's not going to mean what you think it means."

Elefante

NAVIGATE USING NATURE'S COMPASS

>> Look inside the official survival guide issued to British military aircrew and you'll find a neat rule. If you're at sea and, in a five-minute window you see ten birds or more, you're within 40 miles (64km) of land; if you see two birds or fewer, you're more than 40 miles (64km) from land. This simple formula was discovered by Tristan Gooley, a leading expert and bestselling author on "natural navigation," the art of getting from A to B using clues in the environment.

Gooley, the only living person to have crossed the Atlantic solo by both air and sea, started out as an explorer using standard navigation methods. But the more ambitious his expeditions became, the more he found himself relying on technology. "I can remember sitting in an aircraft surrounded by computer screens and dials, and thinking, 'This isn't the thing that really lights my fire,'" he recalls. By chance, he had already heard about the idea of finding one's way using nature and thought he would try it out. "It was like a cerebral bomb going off. I'd come back from a thousand-mile expedition, having felt that it was interesting and challenging, then I'd go and do one mile across some woods using natural navigation and think it was absolutely mind-blowing."

He was converted, and subsequently amassed a vast body of knowledge drawing on everything from ancient Viking texts to modern science journals, filtered through his own experiments. Gooley's techniques, which he has catalogued in books such as *How To Read Water* (2016), are not only useful in an emergency, he says, but also bring an inherent satisfaction that can enhance any trip outdoors. Here are five...

1: LOOK TO THE TREES

If one side of a tree is heavier and denser, with more horizontal branches, that's the side that's getting more sun. If you are in the northern hemisphere, therefore, that's the southern side. (If you're south of the equator, you'll need to switch south for north in this and all subsequent instructions.) The leaves on the shadier, north side of the tree tend to be bigger and darker. "The tree sends a chemical to those leaves saying, 'Pull your socks up,'" explains Gooley. "So they effectively spread themselves out to create a bigger solar panel."

2: CONSIDER THE NETTLE

Stinging nettles are a sign that civilization is nearby. "We think they grow everywhere, but that's because they grow where we are," says Gooley. "Stinging nettles need phosphate-rich soil, and human beings make the soil rich in phosphate through the ways we farm, live, work and die." Wildlife can indicate the proximity of nettles. In Britain, say, the common peacock butterfly — characterized by red wings, black markings and bright eyespots — depends on nettles to survive while in caterpillar form.

3: BY THE LIGHT OF THE MOON

Imagine a line connecting the tips of the Moon's crescent and follow it down to the horizon. This point is approximately south. "Every phase of the Moon is effectively it saying to us, 'This is my current relationship with the Sun,'" explains Gooley. The side of the Moon that is illuminated indicates whether the Sun is to its east or west. A tangent along the "tips" of the Moon will therefore be at 90 degrees to this east-west line and is thus a north-south line.

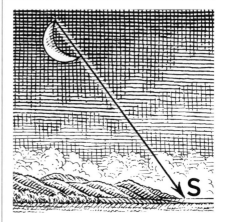

»» 4: IT'S WRIT IN WATER

If you see puddles forming generally on one side of a track, that's likely to be the southern side. A bank on the edge of the path, or any adjacent foliage, will cast a northward shadow when the Sun comes out after a shower, meaning that rainwater takes longer to dry out. "The mud stays soft, so when people move through there's more erosion and the cycle repeats," says Gooley. "Day in day out, over months, that creates puddles."

5: AND IF YOU'RE IN TOWN...

Look for satellite television dishes. These have to point to a geostationary satellite, and for a satellite to stay at the same point over the Earth, it must be over the equator. That means that dishes point broadly south. A little local knowledge can refine this further. "In the UK, for instance, most people rely on Sky for their satellite TV," says Gooley. "That uses a particular satellite group, the Astra 2, which happens to be south-southeast of the country."

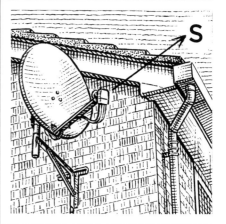

TAKE A "WOW" HOLIDAY PHOTO

» In 2013, Lauren Bath took a gamble. The young Australian chef was working in a restaurant on Queensland's Gold Coast and had just endured a particularly difficult New Year's Eve service. Deciding enough was enough, she quit. On the side, she had been developing her talents as a travel photographer and hit the road determined to turn her art into her full-time job. The plan worked. Now, Bath has a social-media following of around half a million, has been featured in *National Geographic*, and counts Olympus and Moët & Chandon among her clients. So, in an age when camera phones have made photographers of us all, how do you take a holiday shot that stands out?

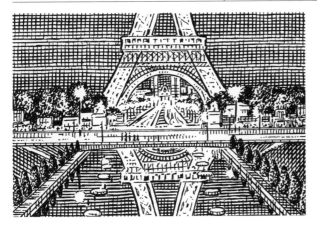

1: GO IN BLIND

On holiday you'll naturally want to shoot the famous sights, but you need to find your own take on them. "The best way to shoot a cliché subject is to minimize how many shots you look at before you go to shoot it. If you pore over hundreds of pictures beforehand, you'll find it very challenging to think of something new," says Bath. "Another good tip is not to settle for the first shot you take. I always call that the safety shot, and it's never my favorite. I try all different things: different focal length on my lenses, different vantage points, reflections..."

2: DITCH THE SELFIE STICK

Selfies, in the usual sense, leave a lot to be desired. If you want to take a self-portrait, it's much better to find a scene that's interesting in its own right but which would be enhanced by a human element in the shot. "To pull off these kinds of selfies, you'll need a tripod and a self-timer. You get your camera and settings all ready to go and manually focus your lens on the place you intend to sit. Set your timer for enough time to allow you to get into frame, push the shutter button and get among it."

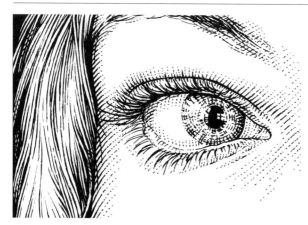

3: PORTRAITS ARE PRIMARILY ABOUT THE EYES

"I always focus on the eyes of my model. If their face isn't level, then it would be the eye closest to me. I want the eyes to be the sharpest point of the whole image." Bath emphasizes that focal point by blurring out the background. A camera phone can do this digitally; a traditional camera requires the lens being set to a low "f-stop" (for a wide aperture). Her second tip for portraits is to shoot with backlight. "That is when your subject is between your camera and your light source — usually the sun. You can get incredible flare and effects with practice."

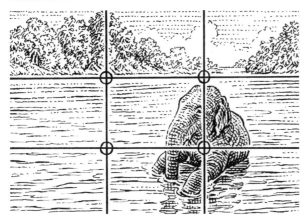

4: LEARN THESE TWO CLASSIC COMPOSITIONAL TECHNIQUES

The "rule of thirds" is an easy way to enhance almost any shot. "Imagine your frame is split into three sections horizontally and vertically. If you have a point of interest, such as a subject, leading line or horizon, try positioning it on one of these lines." Another helpful technique is 'framing'. "This is blocking part of the scene you're shooting with a natural frame in the foreground. You can use doorways or windows, or think outside the box: trees, or portholes on a ship."

5: SHOOT EARLY OR LATE

The optimum times to take photos are the hour after sunrise and the hour before sunset — these are known as golden hours. "When the sun is close to the horizon, this results in soft, warm light. It should make your images look amazing with little extra effort." You should also take a break at midday. "The trickiest time of day to shoot is midday on a sunny or cloudless day, as it is bright and there's a lot of contrast. You'll notice hard shadows everywhere, and shooting people is next to impossible unless you get them in the shade."

6:

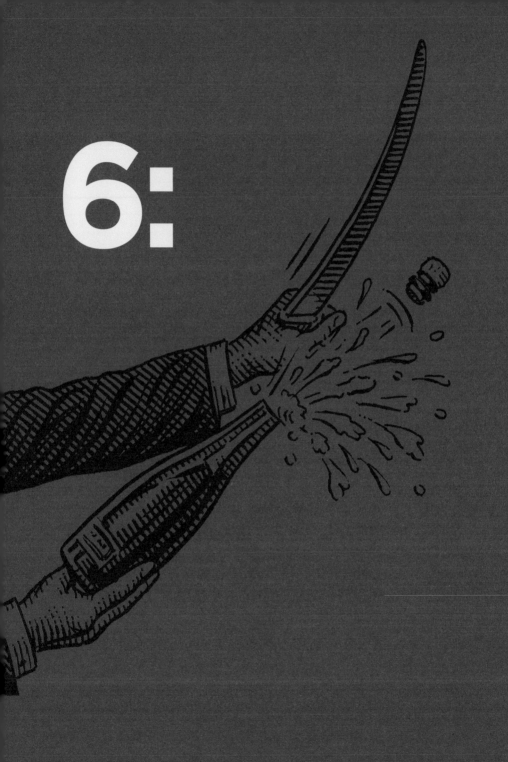

SHOWING OFF

This chapter is all about flourishes and displays. Some of them are party tricks — and a man should always have a few of these in his locker. Performing a jaw-dropping card illusion or diving elegantly into a pool might not have a larger purpose beyond spectacle, but they'll certainly draw plaudits. A number of them, however, will enhance your life in a more permanent way. Tracey Emin's advice on displaying artwork will make your home a better place to be, and our guide to developing an amazing memory will augment much of your day-to-day...

PERFORM MIND-BLOWING MAGIC LIKE DYNAMO

>> There was a time when magic was seen as a novelty act. Then the likes of Dynamo (a.k.a. Steven Frayne) came along. His award-winning illusions, which have awed everyone from Pharrell Williams to Brad Pitt, are unlike traditional magic in that they aren't about "fooling" people. "It's more about sharing a moment," says the magician, who recently published *Dynamo: The Book of Secrets* (2017), "and creating a memory." We asked him for a trick that's guaranteed to impress...

The trick:

A participant selects a card.

They replace it, then shuffle the pack face up and face down.

The deck is spread. The face-up cards are a phone number. They dial it, and are told to ask whoever answers to name their card. Your phone rings, and you give them the answer...

1: SET THE DECK

Before the trick starts, riffle through the deck and create a packet of cards corresponding to your phone number. Use aces for ones and queens for zeros (Q looks like 0). The card at the back of the packet ought to represent the first digit; in our illustration we are using the example number 07225 386491. Place these cards face down on the top of the deck. Dynamo says that you can get away with doing this prep in front of the participant. "If I'm just casually messing with the cards as I talk to you, you're not going to be that concerned with what's going on."

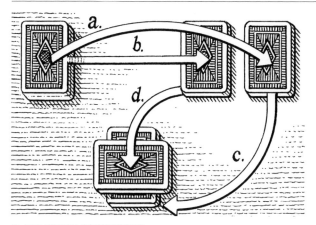

2: TIME TO PERFORM

First, force the participant to choose a predesignated card. Here's the simplest method. Put the deck on the table, noting the bottom card. Ask the participant to cut the deck. Say: "Let's mark where you cut," and place the bottom half on the top half to make a cross. Talk for a while, distracting them from which half was which. Tell them to pick up the (new) top half, turn it over and, "Remember the card you cut to but don't show me". In reality, they're looking at the card that you noted at the start.

3: MAKE THE PACKETS

Say: "Now, you're going to mix these cards up completely, so that some are facing one way and some are facing the other." Spread the cards in your hands and remove only the cards containing your phone number. Place these face down on the table (packet 1 in the picture). Take another packet of 10–15 cards and place them face up to their right (2). Place a third set face down to the right of those (3). The remainder should go face up on the far right (4).

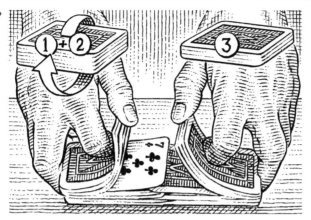

4: SHUFFLE UP

Push packets (1) and (2) across for them to riffle shuffle (interleave) together. Take back the combined packet (1+2). Say: "Now you're going to do it again," turning over (1+2) as you talk. Push (1+2) and (3) across for shuffling and take back (1+2+3). Turn (1+2+3) over as you tidy it up. Push this and (4) across for a final shuffle. When you take the cards back, turn them over one last time. The ones you placed on the top of the deck at the start will be face up, but the participant won't have realized that.

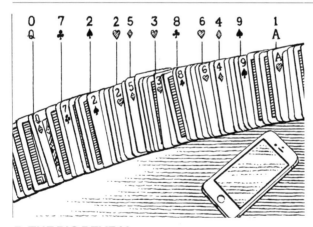

5: THE BIG REVEAL

Say: "I'm going to turn all the cards back around except yours." Spread the cards on the table. A variety of them – your ones – will be face up, as per step 4. Pretend the trick hasn't worked. Say: "OK, let's try another way." Ask them to type the numbers of the face-up cards into their phone, helping them translate cards into digits as they go. Say: "Dial it and ask whoever picks up to name your card." Your phone will ring; reveal their card. Good vibes? Save their phone number.

DIVE INTO A POOL GRACEFULLY

>> Once a pool party starts, so the diving competition inevitably follows, and whoever can actually pull off something half decent is, for that one, beautiful moment, a legend — because an elegant dive is an especially crowd-pleasing sight, as the young Tom Daley quickly learned. "I used to find it quite funny that people were so mesmerized by something I found so easy," he says. Admittedly, Daley had rather a knack for it. At 15, he became Britain's first individual world diving champion and went on to win two Olympic medals. His first piece of advice is hard-won. "Check the depth of the pool," he says. "I once chipped my teeth on the bottom." The ideal depth for a low springboard is at least 3m (10ft). And to develop an ideal dive...

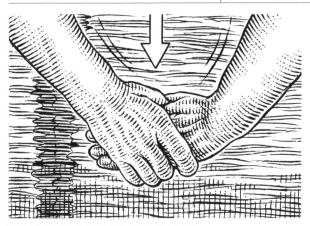

1: LEARN THE DIVER'S CLASP

Contrary to popular belief, divers enter the water with their hands clasped as shown. The idea is to land with your palms facing the water to create as big a surface area as possible, with your arms squeezing tightly against your ears. Get used to this by standing on the edge of the pool, as if about to dive. "Bend over as far as you can with your legs straight and your hands clasped. Lift up on to your toes and just fall in," he says. "Your legs will follow and go up — it will happen without you knowing it."

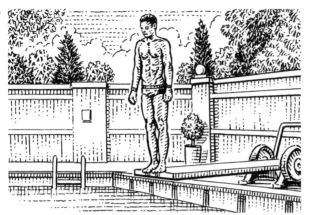

2: GET THE STANCE

Time to dive properly. When you're standing on the edge of the board, look forward, with your arms by your sides, and adopt a perfectly straight body posture. "That means having your legs completely tight — engaged quads, glutes — and making sure that your pelvic floor is tilted so all your lower abs are engaged," says Daley. That's vital for entering the water stylishly. "The position you start in is often the position that you finish in." Your big toes should be just over the edge.

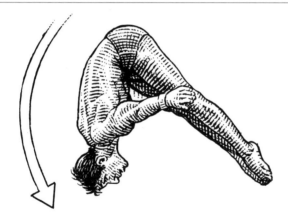

3: HIT THE PIKE

To dive in the correct trajectory, imagine that you're jumping up and over a waist-height fence. As you jump, bring your arms up into a "T." At the apex, do a "pike" (see picture) where you bend forward at the hips. "Then all you have to do is engage your glutes and squeeze, and that will lift your legs up pretty quickly." Once your body has straightened out, clasp your hands as per step 1. A common mistake is to forget to focus on keeping your legs together. To fix that, practice diving while holding a towel between your ankles. "The aim is to keep it between your legs until you hit the water."

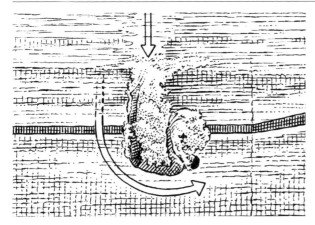

4: THE RIP ENTRY

Ever wondered how divers such as Daley enter the water with hardly a splash? That clasped-hands position is key. As soon as the water is up to your ears, flick your wrists apart and open your arms up into a "T." "It creates a vacuum which sucks the water underneath with you." To further eliminate splash, wait until your shins are about to go under and hinge at the hips for a forward roll. "Rolling contains all of the water and air that gets brought under with you, so it helps with the perfect entry."

5: TAKE IT FURTHER

Once you've nailed a basic dive, learn to do a simple forward somersault. Stand on the edge of the pool, with your arms up but not joined, and jump up and out. "The key, now, is to pretend you're throwing a boulder. You bend your arms slightly behind your head and when you 'throw,' your hips will come up and over your head," says Daley. At that point, go into a "tuck" — this is like a cannonball but with one hand on each of your shins – before landing on your feet. "You'll turn over easier than you thought."

PSYCH OUT YOUR POKER OPPONENT

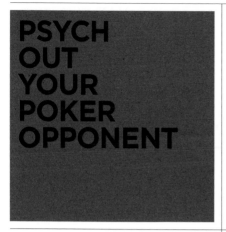

>> When the poker film *Rounders* came out in 1998, it ushered a new wave of players to the card table. It also introduced those players to the notion of "chip tricks" — the nimble-fingered manipulation of gambling chips to exude confidence and intimidate weaker players. In a memorable scene, Matt Damon's character plays against the real-life multiple World Series of Poker champion Johnny Chan, who flourishes his chips with a move that remains popular today, known simply as "the Johnny Chan." Next game, why not try it?

1: GET STACKED

Pick up a number of chips as shown — between six and ten should do.

2: LIFT OFF

Use your thumb to roll the front three chips upward to your index finger.

3: CHIP AWAY

Drop the front chip, positioning your middle and ring fingers to guide it back to the stack.

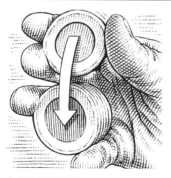

4: FINISH IT

Follow through with the other two chips, like an overhand shuffle. Repeat, menacingly.

EXECUTE THE ZIPPO SNAP

>> Granted, you don't smoke — but that's no reason not to own a lighter. There's a worldliness in being able to start a campfire, put a flame on a dinner candle or do the required when someone asks you for a light. A metal, Zippo-style number is what you need — and the slickest way to strike it? Look no further than how Ryan Gosling wields his for Emma Stone in *Gangster Squad* (2013). He sparks it up with just enough flare to cut a dash; anything more complex would look too studied and, therefore, unstylish. Here's the move...

1: ALL IN HAND
Produce your lighter, holding it as shown with its hinge to the left.

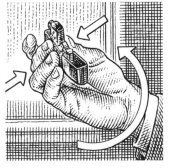

2: PING THE LID
Snap your thumb and fingers together while rotating the hand through 90 degrees.

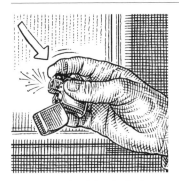

3: MAKE SPARKS FLY
Strike the flint wheel, straighten the lighter and present the flame.

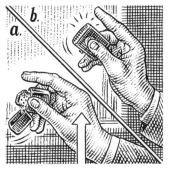

4: CLOSING TIME
Turn the lighter horizontal again and whip your hand to snap it shut.

SABRE A CHAMPAGNE BOTTLE

>> Legend has it that, during the early part of the Napoleonic Wars, the French cavalry would celebrate their victories by slicing open champagne bottles with their sabres. And so, "sabrage" was born. "It was then copied by the British, by the King's German Legion, by the Russians," says Julian White. "But it stopped after the Battle of Waterloo as obviously there was no more fighting." In 1986, the Confrérie du Sabre d'Or, for which White is Ambassador Emeritus, was set up to repopularize the art. Here's his guide...

1: LOWER THE TEMPERATURE

Chill a champagne bottle. "A fridge is 5°C (about 40°F), which is cold enough, but if you want to have a really clean cut and not lose a lot of spume, chill the bottle in the deep freeze for about ten minutes." Next, remove the wire cage and foil around the cork.

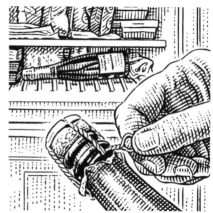

2: CLEAR A PATH

Find the vertical seam where the glass joins. Expose a strip in the neck foil so you can see the full line. "The seam, generally speaking, is where the foil comes together, so you can just turn the foil back on both sides."

3: PRESENT ARMS

Put your thumb in the base of the bottle, and cradle it at 45 degrees with your fingers. Ensure there's nobody in the line of fire. Position a blunt sabre — or, failing that, the blunt edge of a kitchen knife — a few inches from the base of the bottle. Hold the blade flat against the seam.

4: SABRE AWAY

Run the blade up the seam. The impact of the metal against the lip of the bottle will cause the cork and the glass around it to fly off. "Go straight through and don't stop. You don't need a lot of testosterone; it should be an elegant sweep."

5: AFTER NOTES...

While sweeping the blade, it should never lose contact with the glass. "If you 'chop down' even a millimeter on to the glass at the end of the bottle, it will explode." Also, avoid sabring clear bottles, as the glass may be too weak. And pour the champagne immediately — well, do you want a warm drink?

TURBO-CHARGE YOUR MEMORY

>> Could you recite pi to 4,100 decimal places? Dominic O'Brien can. The eight-times winner of the World Memory Championships can also memorize the order of 54 packs of playing cards shuffled together; he can recall the names of 100 previously unseen faces after just 15 minutes of study; and he keeps every appointment without the need of a diary. Yet he says there's nothing special about his mind. In fact, all his feats are based on a few simple principles, which he regularly teaches to actors struggling to learn lines and to foreign dignitaries who wish to speak without notes. "There's a misconception that there is only a finite amount of information you can remember before you fill up your 'memory banks.' That's nonsense," he says. "The more you train your memory, the easier it is to memorize information."

1: MAKE AN IMAGE

To remember a sequence, you need to visualize each item as an image. For objects, this is straightforward — but you must imagine them with all your senses and try to make them more memorable by giving them unusual details. For abstract sequences, such as strings of numbers, you have to think laterally. Perhaps 53 can become an image of Eric Clapton, because five and three correspond to E and C in the alphabet. O'Brien's book *You Can Have an Amazing Memory* (2011) details various systems for you to borrow. Now, you need to combine the images.

2: THE JOURNEY METHOD

You need to place each item at a stop on a familiar journey that you can visualize in your mind. Imagine walking around your house. The stops might be: bedroom, landing, bathroom, kitchen, front door. If the first item on the list is an axe, imagine that there is an axe lodged in your bedroom wardrobe. If the next is a car, imagine walking on to the landing and having to squeeze around a roadster. Journeys like this can be used to store everything from shopping lists to the structure of a speech.

3: BUILD A BANK OF JOURNEYS

You may wonder how to avoid being confused by "ghosts" of previous items when memorizing a new list using the same route. The answer is to have at least ten familiar journeys that you can rotate — by the time you use the first one again, you will have forgotten what you stored on it. "I collect journeys," says O'Brien. "I add two or three new journeys every year that I can use for competition or demonstrations." This could be a route around a town, perhaps, or a golf course. The best journeys are those you know without hesitation, involve indoor and outdoor spaces, and have a significance for you.

4: THE RULE OF FIVE

If you are remembering a large data set that you wish to use for a long time — O'Brien once learned forty years' worth of number one singles — you need to repeat the memorizing process. "Through experience I've noticed that I need to do that five times."

Ideally, you would study the information and then review it immediately, and once again 24 hours later. Revisit it a third time four to seven days after that, and a fourth time after a month. The final review should happen three to six months later.

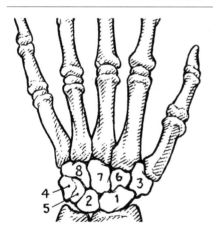

1. Scaphoid
2. Lunate
3. Trapezium
4. Pisiform
5. Triquetrum
6. Trapezoid
7. Capitate
8. Hamate

5: AN EXTRA TOOL

The journey method is a powerful tool, but mnemonics can also prove useful. "This tends to be quite popular with medical students who have to remember quite difficult Latin terms." "Some Lovers Try Positions That They Can't Handle," for example, is a mnemonic for the carpal bones:

Scaphoid, Lunate, Trapezium, Pisiform, Triquetrum, Trapezoid, Capitate and Hamate. And if you need to remember a large number of acronyms? Store images of them on a journey, of course.

WIN AT KICK-UPS

>> Jermaine Jenas says that kick-ups are becoming a lost art in professional soccer. Once athletes reach the top tier, the focus shifts to strength and speed — no time for what seems like a childish trick. "I've come across players who would openly say, 'I can't do 50 kick-ups, that's not part of my game,'" he says. To Jenas, a former England international and now soccer pundit on British television, that's regrettable. Sure, juggling a ball around your body looks impressive — but it can also train you in vital aspects of the sport. Brazil is one of the few countries where players keep drilling kick-ups, and their track record speaks for itself. "I watch the training now and the fundamentals of what they do are head tennis and beach volleyball with their feet — juggling the ball."

Jenas believes that his career, which started at Nottingham Forest and took him to Newcastle United, Tottenham Hotspur, Aston Villa and Queen's Park Rangers, directly benefited from obsessively practicing kick-ups while growing up in Nottingham. "I would be in the back garden all day and I'd come running in, saying to my mum or dad, 'I've done 80 kick-ups!' They'd say, 'Do it again...'" Not only does the skill teach control, balance and technique, it also helps you learn to use both feet — and develop a useful competitive streak. "The fundamentals of it are what create soccer players, in the end." Despite being out of the game since the 2013–14 season, today he can easily still do 100 kick-ups. With these tips (and practice), you can too...

» 1: LET IT OUT

If you're a beginner, you need to lower the difficulty. Practice on hard ground and, more importantly, deflate the ball just a little. "If you watch all these skillsters on YouTube, and they're doing all these tricks, their balls are not fully pumped up."

2: KNOW THYSELF

Poise the ball on top of your foot. Where it naturally sits is your sweet spot. When you start practicing, this is the part of the foot that should connect with the ball. You should also train your overall stability. "Try standing on one leg while covering an eye — it will throw you off massively."

3: THE ACTION ITSELF

Think of it less as a kick than a flick, and always point your toe slightly upward to ensure the ball doesn't fly off. "The lower you can keep the ball, the more control you'll have over it. You don't want to go any higher than your knee." Keep those knees bent and joints loose.

4: HOW TO TRAIN

Drop the ball and let it bounce. Kick it up, let it bounce and kick it up again. Keep repeating this pattern until you're confident enough to try two kicks prior to each bounce. Build up from there. Don't omit to train your weaker foot, too. "The quicker you can get to using two feet, the better."

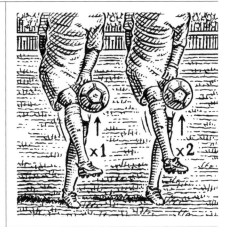

5: TAKE IT FURTHER

When you can do lots of kick-ups, experiment with feeding the ball up to other parts of your body such as your head. Jenas's tip for sets of headers: don't just use your neck, or you won't get enough power. "You need to use your hips to generate thrust with your shoulders and head."

SING LIKE A STAR

>> In 2017, the music blog Pitchfork ran a piece headlined, "Jorja Smith has a voice that could heal the world." A voice, it went on to observe, that is "soothing and substantial... filled with an aching that suggests she was born to counsel the world's suffering." The writer was not alone in her adulation. The soul/R&B singer has won plaudits across the industry, from Drake (who Instagram-messaged her, asking to collaborate) to radio and TV presenter Nick Grimshaw (who called her "his favorite British voice since Amy Winehouse") via Kendrick Lamar (who enlisted her for his 2018 all-star *Black Panther* album). At 2018's BRIT Awards, she justifiably picked up the coveted Critics' Choice gong. Here, Smith and her vocal coach Emma Stevens offer a masterclass in singing like a star...

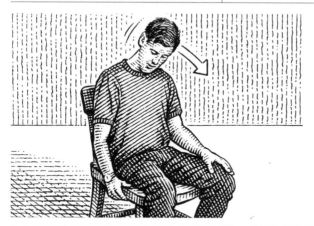

1: WARM UP YOUR VOCAL CHORDS — AND EVERYTHING ELSE

Before a show, Smith begins by finding a soprano warm-up video readily available online — that provides music for singing words such as "kiu" and "ning" at different pitches. "It's twenty minutes and I do that," she says. It's also important to stretch. Sit down on a chair and lock one arm under the seat, then tip your head to the opposite shoulder while keeping your chin tucked in. To loosen up the mouth, imagine you're using your tongue to get toffee out of your back teeth. Also, try standing up and shaking out your whole body.

2: FORGET EVERYTHING YOU KNOW ABOUT BREATHING

"If you watch Céline Dion or Beyoncé — their upper chest won't move very much, their breath is coming from very low in their body," says Stevens. "That is crucial, because if your breathing is shallow, you'll have a situation where you get tension up in the neck and jaw, and that will create vocal damage very quickly." To learn how to breathe the right way, "Imagine a balloon behind your belly button, and that you're sucking air through a straw directly into that balloon. That is a singer's breath."

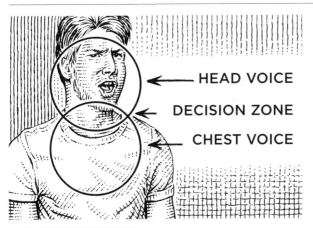

HEAD VOICE ←

DECISION ZONE ←

CHEST VOICE ←

3: SHIFT THE VOICE

"Don't sing from your throat," says Smith. "You have to sing from your diaphragm." However, you will notice that notes of different pitches resonate in different places: lower notes resonate in your chest ("chest voice"), while higher ones resonate in your head ("head voice"). For the notes in the middle, you have to decide which voice to use — and that choice will let you achieve particular effects. If you go high in your chest voice, you can belt like Chuck Berry. Equally, says Smith, "Sometimes I'm not going to belt it if it would sound awful, so I would do head voice."

4: BEWARE THE NOSE

"Don't sing through your nose," says Smith. "A lot of people do. I used to — my Dad used to tell me off for it." The problem with doing this is that it can make you sound squeaky, like a Disney character. That said, if you're careful, using the nose in moderation can be helpful. "It can put an edge on a breathy sound," says Stevens. "So if Jorja wants a little bit more power up there, I would say, 'Put it in your nose a little bit.' But she has to be very careful it doesn't turn into a chipmunk sound. It's a balance."

5: SMILE!

"If you smile, it makes you open your mouth while you're singing," says Smith. It also lifts up the soft palate at the back of the mouth, which is crucial for resonance and tone; if it's dropped, then you'll get a deader, flatter sound. The sound itself, however, should feel like it's at the front of the mouth. "Imagine that your voice is hitting the back of your front teeth," says Stevens. "That will bring your voice forward into the harder space." If you do that, you won't need to stretch your jaw wide like a chorister. And on stage, you don't want to look like a chorister.

HANG ART ON YOUR WALLS LIKE AN ARTIST

» The British art superstar Tracey Emin made her name with autobiographical work that doesn't pull its punches. There's *My Bed* (1998), the installation that was shortlisted for the Turner Prize in 1999, for instance, and *Everyone I Have Ever Slept With 1963–1995* (1995), a tent appliquéd with names. Her opinions on buying art are no less direct. "Some people buy art that they don't understand, that they don't feel for, but they've been told it's the right thing to do and it matches their status. That's a big mistake," she says. "The best reason is that it makes you feel different, makes you feel more imaginative, more loving, more passionate, more intellectual, more poetic." Once you have something you love, here's her advice for presenting it in the home...

1: REFRAME WITH CAUTION

"One mistake that people often make is they change the frame that the artist put on. You shouldn't do that. The artist chose that frame because the artist felt that's what the work should have. If you want to change the frame, you should ask the artist — not ask their permission, but explain that you'd like to have something else and discuss it with them." That said, keep in mind that reframing can devalue the piece. Bonus tip: if you want to reframe an old painting in a more contemporary fashion, put it in a brushed-steel tray frame with a gap of 3–4mm (about ⅒in) around the canvas.

2: THINK ABOUT THE SPACE AS MUCH AS THE ART

While it can work to hang a piece that dominates a room — that is, if the interior design is relatively minimalist — you should beware of allowing a room to overpower the art. "You can have a really tiny work on a wall and it looks hideous, because it looks like a hole in the wall." And sometimes deciding where not to hang is just as important. "In my bedroom at home I have no art at all, nor in my bedroom in New York nor my bedroom in France. I just like to have clear space, I like to wake up with my own thoughts."

3: PUT IT AT THE RIGHT HEIGHT

"155 to 160cm [61 to 63in] is the usual height for the center of the piece to be at eye level. But often that's too high. If it's a small work, you want it to be lower — you want to be able to look into it. Things are normally hung for the heights of men and not for the heights of women." You can also think about hanging things in extreme places to achieve a dramatic effect. "You can hang things at different heights depending on what it is. Some things can just look really cool hung low or really high in the corner."

4: CHOOSE SUITABLE CONDITIONS

Don't put artwork in direct sunlight — that's why north light is often used in galleries. "The thing you mustn't ever have in direct sunlight is photographs because they'll disappear within six months to a year." Also, think carefully before putting something up in the bathroom. It won't last long, and besides, is it necessary? "I always look at the art in the [British Airways] Concorde Lounge, in the toilets, and I think why do they do that, do we really need to look at a Peter Doig when we're on the toilet?"

5: TRY A SALON HANG

This is when you put lots of pictures on a wall, just like in a 19th-century salon. But you need to plan it out first. "You lay it out on the floor next to the wall you want to do it on. Say your biggest picture is going to go in the middle to the left, you put that on the floor in the middle to the left, and you just do it from there by eye." When it comes to putting them on the wall, don't worry too much about the distance between pictures. "You don't have to measure it all out," she says. "But you need at least 4cm [1½in] or 5cm [2in] between each work so it can breathe a little bit."

7:

WORK & CAREER

Going to work is never just about doing your job. You have to learn a whole other set of skills in order to survive and thrive in the workplace. Nobody's going to give you a pay rise unless you ask for one, so how best to negotiate it? When you need to present a new product or talk at a leaving party, how do you do that with charisma? And when you've been told to take on an extra project, how do you get it done? We consulted the specialist in those areas and more. If an office job isn't your speed, don't worry — we've got a guide to writing a bestselling novel, too...

START A BILLION-DOLLAR COMPANY

>> Sir Richard Branson's empire of more than 400 companies, 90,000 staff and a private island began with just under $300. That was the money he put into *Student* magazine, which he set up at the age of 16 to give young people a voice at the height of the Vietnam War. From there he became a paragon of entrepreneurialism, founding a chain of record stores (and, later, a record label), an airline, a train company, a radio station, a series of gyms, a space tourism operation — all under the Virgin umbrella. Today, Virgin Group is worth an estimated $7 billion and Branson is one of the most influential people on the planet. We asked him for the crucial advice you must heed to ensure your next business venture flourishes...

1: FRUSTRATIONS ARE A GREAT SOURCE OF BUSINESS IDEAS

"I hated flying on other people's airlines," says Branson. "The experience was a miserable one, there was no entertainment, the food was dreadful, the staff generally didn't smile, they were old planes. So, out of sheer frustration, I thought, 'Let's get a secondhand 747 and give it a go,' and Virgin Atlantic was born. With Virgin Records, it was out of frustration at not being able to get a record deal for Mike Oldfield's *Tubular Bells*. I knew it was a great, beautiful-sounding record, but nobody would sign it. So I said: 'Screw that, let's start our own record company.'"

2: YOUR PRODUCT MUST BE BETTER THAN YOUR COMPETITORS'

"We've had a number of things that haven't worked out — obviously Virgin Cola was the biggest one. But we had a lot of fun doing it and it didn't do us any harm: if you take on the big guys and fail, people respect you for it. The principal thing I learned from it was we weren't different enough. We had a fun brand but we were just a can of cola. Ever since then we've never launched anything unless we feel that we are head and shoulders above the competition."

3: EMBRACE FLEXIBLE WORKING

"You've got to get a fantastic team around you and, in my opinion, treat them like you would your family. In Virgin Group headquarters, people can take as much holiday as they want and it's paid. If people want to work from home, they can work from home. I've always worked from either a houseboat or an island — I've never worked from an office, and I'm sitting here now in a hammock looking over the sea and running a small empire with 90,000 people. Working from a pleasant environment, you can get more done and have more time to think."

4: CARRY A NOTEBOOK

"I'm a bit religious about it. If I'm on a Virgin plane, I will get out there, talk to the staff, talk to the customers, and it's that feedback that ends up making a company exceptional. If you don't write things down, you don't get them sorted. If I'm in a meeting with people and they're not taking notes, I may not show it but I get slightly frustrated. A lot of people feel that taking notes is beneath them, that it's somehow not something that chief execs at companies do. But I think they're mistaken."

5: DELEGATE, DELEGATE, DELEGATE

Rather than getting bogged down in the day-to-day, you need to be free to look at the big picture (though be prepared to get involved when there's a problem). "I've told a lot of entrepreneurs: once you've got the company up and running, replace yourself in the office and move out of the office. Let that person run the company. And then, because you're not there, you're not going to offend anybody if someone turns up wanting to see you and take up your time. If you're a real entrepreneur, you'll be moving on to the next entrepreneurial excitement."

WORK A ROOM LIKE A MASTER CONNECTOR

>> Networking is officially a turn-off. A study by University of Toronto has shown that the mere mention of business cards or professional networks is sufficient to induce feelings of disgust — and yet those same researchers also found that networking is vital for getting ahead in your career. The key, according to Oli Barrett, is to change how you approach it.

Barrett was once anointed "the most connected man in Britain" by *Wired* magazine. The co-founder of social innovation agency Cospa has led 11 international trade missions, sits on multiple advisory boards, including that of the Center for Entrepreneurs, and is credited with bringing speed networking to the UK. We asked him for five cast-iron tips to make networking more natural, more enjoyable and more effective...

1: DON'T GO IN COLD TO AN EVENT

Research the other guests and, if out of town, skim the local newspaper — it's a great source of titbits, and your awareness will impress. Also consider how you're going to introduce yourself. The key is to offer an array of hooks to get the conversation rolling. "I met a guy who realized the way he had been introducing himself was too boring — just his name and what he did. By giving a longer introduction — that he was from New Zealand, that he had stayed there for a long time as he loves surfing, but now he's in California — he could offer four or five talking points."

2: DON'T BE WEIRD

While you can simply walk up to guests, your opener should call out what you're doing: "Do you mind if I introduce myself?" It's preferable, however, to be introduced by the host. "You can say to her, 'This is a brilliant event, all sorts of interesting people — who's here?' That has given me higher-quality introductions than anything else." Having met someone, don't ask, "What do you do?" Many people hate their job and the question can imply judgment. Instead, try, "What's keeping you busy at the moment?"

3: DON'T BE A BUSINESS CARD BUFFOON

Never hand over your business card at the start or end of a conversation. "To me, that's a bit salesman. My ideal time is at a particular point where you've identified a mutual interest — 'I'd be very pleased to drop you a note about that.'" That approach is especially beneficial, as networking is all about showing you can be helpful to someone, thereby building goodwill for the future. Barrett likes to have a set of personal business cards alongside company cards. The former are practical (if he changes job, he won't lose the contact) and also make the other person feel special.

4: DON'T FLUFF THE EXIT

Room-working newbies often find it awkward to leave a conversation. A good tactic is to introduce the other person to someone else, and then say goodbye. However, it's also perfectly acceptable to be more straightforward. Barrett's favorite line is: "I know you've probably got other people you want to meet. Will you excuse me, I've just got to go and say hello to a colleague?" You can then sign off with: "Are you staying for the rest of the evening? I might see you later on."

5: DON'T MISTAKE WORKING A ROOM FOR NETWORKING

Want to create a connection with someone? Follow up. Offering to meet near their office for a 20-minute coffee is effective, as are brief handwritten notes. "I know someone who sold a company for over a billion dollars. The secret of their success was sending handwritten notes to investors they met along the way." More importantly, maintain connections. If Barrett sees an interesting news article, he sends it to at least two people with a message saying, "I saw this and thought of you. No need to reply." He also has Google alerts to prompt him to write when someone has had good (or bad) news.

ASK FOR A PAY RAISE — AND GET IT

>> Think you're a good negotiator? You may be wrong. Adam Grant argues that even experts use strategies that, although widely perceived to be effective, are actually counterproductive. A professor at the Wharton School, University of Pennsylvania, and the author of *Give and Take* (2013), Grant uses data-led research to establish tactics that actually work — and has taught his findings to major organizations such as the US Army, World Economic Forum and Google. We asked him for the most fruitful way to handle that necessary but difficult conversation: asking your boss for a higher salary...

1: BEFOREHAND, WORK OUT WHAT YOU WANT

Establish a target salary range based on industry benchmarks and — if possible — the revenue you create for the business. Also, calculate the value of your next best alternative to a raise, such as taking a job elsewhere. "Then you won't accept anything worse than your backup."

2: IN THE MEETING, CREATE A MOOD OF COLLABORATION

Build rapport, sharing information that can't be used against you. When it's time to talk salary, show that you're serious but fair-minded. Grant likes the line: "These are my goals, I'd love to figure out a way to achieve them that's also reasonable for you."

3: DON'T JUST ASK FOR MORE MONEY

Put multiple items on the table — your salary, your job description, perks — in different combinations: "I'd be thrilled with a 20 percent raise and an opportunity to change my title; or a 15 percent raise and a shift in role." As it's no longer a simple "yes" or "no" question, psychologically your boss is more likely to choose one of your options — all of which involve a raise.

4: THE NEGOTIATION

Justify your demands based primarily on your contribution to the company. If your boss makes you a decent counteroffer, you should still try to nudge him upward. Decrease your initial offer by ever smaller amounts (to suggest that you're nearing a hard line) until you reach agreement.

5: WHAT IF THEY REFUSE TO OFFER ANYTHING AT ALL?

Ask if there is someone else in the company you could speak to. If there isn't, say, "That isn't viable for my long-term plans, so if that's the bottom line, I may have to see what else is available. But I don't want to do that so if there is a way to avoid it, I would love to explore that."

GIVE A SPEECH THAT THEY'LL REMEMBER

>> At the British Conservative Party conference in 1977, a 16-year-old boy stole the show with a stirring speech so accomplished that Margaret Thatcher declared it "thrilling." That boy was William Hague, who would later become a Conservative MP, rise to serve as the party's leader and, in 2015, be made a life peer: Lord Hague of Richmond. His talent for public speaking has underpinned his successes, and he is regarded by many as one of the finest political orators — and, indeed, after-dinner wits — of his generation. The key, he says, is planning every speech. "I don't know if I'm at thousands or tens of thousands, but I still, even now, always prepare, because every audience is different," he says. As for what to prepare, and how to deliver it...

1: THE OPENING IS FUNDAMENTAL

"What goes into the first two minutes is worth ten times more than what goes into the 20th minute," says Lord Hague. That's because people decide whether to listen or tune out right at the start. "There's not a fixed rule to how you begin, but it's got to be something which gets their attention.

The classic way, of course, is with a self-deprecating joke or story that shows that you're not a pompous, arrogant person." He says he has a large stock of stories he likes to pick from: "Embarrassing situations of international diplomacy, rude confrontations with voters..."

2: DON'T JUST PUT PEN TO PAPER

Every speech should have an argument, even a speech at a wedding, so sketch out the structure first. "There is some limit to how many ideas can be in a speech. A rule of three is pretty good." When you start writing, pepper the speech with moments that get the audience to interact — perhaps make them laugh, clap or respond to a question — as this keeps them engaged. "When I was trying to get selected as an MP, my rule was to get the selection committee to 'do something' every 90 seconds."

3: WAKE UP YOUR VOICE

A good start is to get some fresh air. "Before a big conference speech, I would go for a walk on the seafront at Blackpool. Or before Prime Minister's questions, I would always go and walk around St James's Park." A dose of sugar just beforehand also helps. "This can be having a spoonful of sugar in your tea. Or the more decadent version is to have a drink of port, which, having a high sugar content, does actually increase the volume of your larynx. In the House of Commons, when there were 400 Labour MPs against me — and they could make a lot of noise — then I used to have the sugar in the tea."

4: FOCUS ON THE PHYSICAL

Keeping fit is vital. "You need big lungs and that enables you sometimes to give a continuous sentence or paragraph without interrupting your breath — to suddenly do that can be an effective technique." When delivering the speech, project from the chest rather than the throat. You should also aim to convey excitement about what you're saying and make gestures. "You see MPs stick their hands in their pockets. It's distracting to do that, and the body language looks like, 'I don't care about this situation.'"

5: MAKE THE ENDING COUNT

"The value of the ending is that it's probably the bit they are going to remember the most." It should summarize the argument but not repeat it — you could use a new anecdote, say, or new forms of language. If you have a strict time limit, prepare the ending as a separate item to which you can directly jump. Afterward, if appropriate, take questions. This shows that you know your subject matter, and being open to discussion improves the atmosphere in which your speech is received. "Generally, you should overrule anyone who is advising you not to take questions."

ACE THE JOB INTERVIEW

>> When the Bank of England, Stanford University or MetLife need to fill their most senior positions, they call Odgers Berndtson. The high-profile headhunting firm is run by Kester Scrope, and he says that sometimes even the smartest candidates need to brush up on their interview technique. "You would be amazed and appalled by how badly prepared people often are." Research is vital — not only to push the right buttons, but also to find out if you actually want the job in the first place. If the prospect does excite you, here are five tips to avoid common pitfalls...

1: RESEARCH THE PERSON WHO WILL BE INTERVIEWING YOU

"If you can create a sense of empathy by finding common ground with somebody, that is incredibly helpful," says Scrope. "So, if it turns out you went to the same university, when they ask you about your education, you can mention that. They will be flattered that you're interested in them."

2: BE STRATEGIC BUT DON'T DECEIVE

Aim to make a good impression — arrive ten minutes early, prepare a question to ask at the end. Don't, however, pretend to be someone you're not. It's a drain on brainpower, and the truth will out. Similarly, don't exaggerate past successes. "They'll see through it, and it just calls into question everything you're claiming."

» 3: SHOW THAT YOU ARE EXCITED ABOUT THE JOB

"Sometimes people come a cropper because they don't want to look too keen. This comes across as rather haughty. That's a turn-off: it will make the employer concerned you won't stick around. Tell them you're excited about the job, and show that through energy and enthusiasm. They'll want to see those qualities anyway, as they are the key to leading people."

4: PREPARE FOR CLASSIC TRAP QUESTIONS

Example: "What are your weaknesses?" For this one, consider what your referees will say about you when they're asked the same thing. So be honest — though don't choose anything damaging — and, crucially, explain your strategy for offsetting it. You might say: "I get over-commited with work, but my passion for sport helps give me balance."

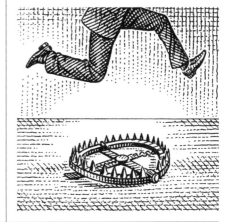

5: RESIST ANSWERING SIMPLE QUESTIONS WITH CLICHÉS

Take: "Why do you want to work here?" Rather than talking about how they're the best in the business, Scrope suggests trying: "The values of the organization fit me and I think you have an amazing opportunity to take the business from A to B. It would be fantastic for my career to be able to be a part of that journey."

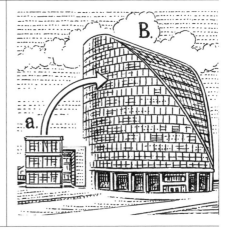

WRITE A BEST-SELLING NOVEL

>> Think it's tough to publish your first book? Tony Parsons has some words of encouragement. "Actually, you're in quite a good position," he says, "because you can be anything — there's no expectation with you." Parsons speaks from experience. While working in a London gin factory as a teenager, he wrote his debut novel, *The Kids* (1976), and was inspired to switch careers. Alongside regular newspaper and magazine columns, he would go on to produce a run of bestsellers, including his breakthrough *Man and Boy* (1999), *The Family Way* (2004) and *My Favorite Wife* (2008), before pivoting into crime fiction with the DC Max Wolfe series, now on its fifth instalment with 2018's *Girl on Fire*. Maintaining such a high hit rate is a function of talent, yes, but also know-how...

1: ONLY WRITE STORIES THAT PASS A CRUCIAL TEST

"What you need to write a successful book is a profound connection to the material," says Parsons. "It doesn't have to be something that happened to you — clearly George R. R. Martin feels a profound connection to *Game of Thrones*." That matters more than novelty. "With *Man and Boy*, it would have been easy to say, 'What's special about this story — guy loses his parents, happens to everybody.' You could talk yourself out of it. But because of that obsessive connection, you make it work." Also ask yourself, "What is this book really about?" and keep the answer in mind as a North Star throughout the writing process.

2: KEEP TO A STRICT SCHEDULE

To kick-start the daunting task of writing a novel, Parsons has a trick. "I write the first line of the book on 1st January, and that's all I have to do that day. It goes back to Hemingway's old mantra for overcoming writer's block: 'All you have to do is write one true sentence.'" He then completes a draft of the first chapter over the following week, and finishes a draft of the book by early summer, working from an outline and a cast list but leaving himself room to improvise. Mornings, he says, are best for writing.

3: EXPERIENCE IS A GREAT RESOURCE — BUT BE DISCERNING

"The mistake that a lot of beginners make is they think that because it happened to them, it's pure gold and that's not necessarily so. Everything must relate to the story." Parsons recounts a vivid childhood memory of going to get a soccer ball from the garage and being struck dumb to find a handgun on the back seat of his father's car. Significant though the moment was, he resisted putting it in *Man and Boy*. "In the context of my childhood it kind of makes sense — my father had this hinterland that I didn't know anything about — but it just didn't work in the story."

4: IT'S NOT ALL ABOUT YOU

"People try to make the lead character them and it doesn't have to be. I think a great example is the way Ian Fleming wrote James Bond. Ian Fleming was not a hero, but he lived his life in the shadow of heroes, so he knew how heroism carried itself. If you read those James Bond books, sometimes it's Fleming's voice — when he's talking about women or patriotism, alcohol or Jamaica — and yet James Bond is not him. I think that works perfectly: when the protagonist is like a shadow brother."

5: GET AN AGENT

When Parsons was 16, and knew that he wanted to be an author, he wrote to famous people for advice. "One person wrote back, and that was Keith Waterhouse. He said, 'Dear Tony, get an agent. Best wishes, Keith.' It was fantastic advice — you're three-quarters of the way home when you've done that." Parsons recommends finding out who represents your favorite authors and writing an attention-grabbing letter to those people, possibly enclosing a chapter of your book. "I'd also say: don't be afraid to fire your agent. A relationship with an agent is like any other, most of them don't end too soon."

HAND-SHAKE YOUR WAY TO SUCCESS

>> It's important to have a good handshake because people don't forget a bad one. "Oxytocin [the social bonding hormone] is released when it's done properly," says Joe Navarro. "We remember bad handshakes because it goes to the same area of the brain where we collect negative information." Navarro honed his body-language expertise as an FBI Special Agent, using his knowledge to catch spies, as detailed in his book *Three Minutes to Doomsday* (2017). Now, he consults on non-verbal communication for the likes of Fortune 500 companies. Here's how to up your handshake game...

1: PRESS THE FLESH

Sweaty palms? "The worst thing you can do is drag your hands down your pants." Instead, adjust your jacket — tug it near the lower button or the lapels — as a way to covertly dry them. This has the bonus of being a "preening" behavior, which elicits positive feelings in others.

2: THE IDEAL HANDSHAKE

Don't get so close that you're invading the other's personal space. Make eye contact, smile and swing your arm in confidently with the fingers angled downward. Engulf their hand warmly, imitating their energy level, and match the pressure to the culture — in Turkey, say, handshakes are weak; in Britain they're firmer. But never crush.

3: TWO TO AVOID

Don't do the politician-style two-hander; if you want to show more affection, grasp their upper arm with your other hand. Also, avoid touching their wrist (a consequence of fingers being angled forward), as this is too intimate. "That leaves you with so many negative feelings."

4: HOW TO GET OUT OF A BAD ONE

If they're not letting you go, respond by briefly squeezing their forearm. "That usually is a good distraction to end the handshaking." Alternatively, if you're getting a knuckle-crusher, call them out. "I've told people, 'Listen, this is not a carnival, you're not going to get a prize from me.'"

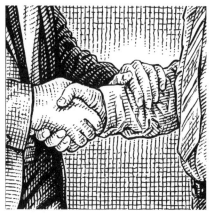

5: BUT IF YOU NEED TO SHOW WHO'S BOSS...

Don't be tempted to start squeezing, pulling or twisting their hand. "I prefer to establish dominance with my body posture and my face. When it's time to terminate the handshake, you'll know it because my countenance will change. The facial muscles will tighten: 'It's time.'"

CONQUER YOUR TO-DO LIST

>> Getting Things Done is the cult productivity system used by Will Smith, Robert Downey Jr and Joss Whedon, among others. It's explained in a 2001 book of the same name that has been bought by more than two million people. The man behind it, David Allen, has been named one of the top five executive coaches in America by *Forbes* magazine. So what exactly is it about GTD that has made this time-management methodology so popular? "Number one," says Allen, "it works." At the core of it is a simple idea: get everything out of your head, so you no longer have to stress about it, and break it all down into manageable tasks. The full system is a complicated beast, so we spoke to Allen about some of its key steps. These alone will help you squeeze even more out of every day...

1: CAPTURE EVERYTHING

Identify all of your "in-baskets" — your email, your physical inbox, your voicemails. GTD says that you must have as few in-baskets as you can get away with. You should also jot down whatever's on your mind — each thing should go on a separate slip of paper. Toss these into your in-tray, too. Ready to process your stuff? Work through your in-baskets systematically from top to bottom. For each item, ask, "Is this actionable?" If it isn't, either discard it or transfer it to a "Someday" list. However, if it is actionable...

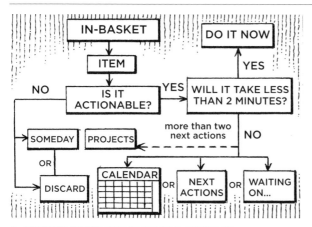

2: WORK OUT THE "NEXT ACTION"

Next actions are the specific, physical things you need to do in order to complete the task. Is the next action doable in less than two minutes? Do it immediately. If not, but it's something you need to do as soon as possible, write it on a "Next Actions" list or — if it's date-specific — put it in your calendar. If a next action is a delegation, however, delegate away and note it on a "Waiting On" list. Any task requiring two or more next actions should also be recorded on a separate "Projects" list.

3: ASSIGN CONTEXTS

You will likely have lots of as-soon-as-possible next actions. "To see all of those at once on a big list would be a little overwhelming," says Allen. So create Next Action lists for different "contexts" — this is the situation in which you'll be best placed to complete the action. For instance, "Commute" might be one, "Computer" or "Home" might be another. Running some errands? Go to your "Errands" list and start working through those. It may also be useful to have people-specific contexts, such as "Boss," for next actions that involve an interaction.

4: FIND TIME TO REFLECT

Once a week, carve out time to review your lists. Ensure that you have removed everything that has been completed. Now go through your Projects, and make sure each has at least one next action. If you encounter a thing that you don't want to do anymore, either get rid of it entirely or shift it to your Someday list. Also consider whether anything from the Someday list should be added to Projects. Some people like to keep a regular slot free every week for this, such as Sunday night.

5: GET A "TICKLER" SYSTEM

A "tickler" system is a way of organizing documents and reminders so that you encounter them on the day they are required. It comprises 43 physical files — one for each day of the month, plus 12 for each month of the year. So: you need to renew your visa on 15th May? Put the application form in the May folder. On the evening of 30th April, take out the May folder and organize its contents into the relevant days. The visa form will go in file 15. Some see the tickler as an optional extra, but Allen says it's vital. "If these things matter to you, you friggin' better have some system."

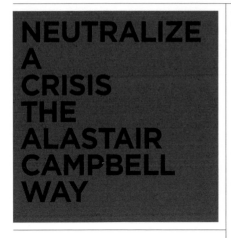

NEUTRALIZE A CRISIS THE ALASTAIR CAMPBELL WAY

» When Alastair Campbell was working for the British Prime Minister Tony Blair—first as his Press Secretary, later as his Director of Communications and Strategy — he managed crises of the highest level. The September 11 attacks, for example, the Kosovo War, the fuel protests and the foot-and-mouth outbreak. Those last two might not have had international ramifications but, as he recalls in his book *Winners* (2015), "they were crises nevertheless, not least because in the early days both gave off signals that the government had lost control and had no answers. Even for non-control freaks, that is quite scary." Yet his record in steering the Labour Party through those experiences — Blair won three general elections — is why Campbell remains in high demand today as a crisis consultant to private organizations and public figures. We asked him what he tells them...

1: QUESTION WHAT YOU'RE DEALING WITH

Ask yourself: is this a crisis, or merely a problem? A crisis, to Campbell, is an event or situation that threatens to overwhelm you if the wrong decisions are taken. Don't go into crisis mode unnecessarily — that can *create* a crisis — but don't be blasé either. "I remember Tony and I were in Canada with Chrétien, the Canadian Prime Minister. Godric Smith, my number two, came into a meeting and gave us a note that said there had been an outbreak of foot-and-mouth. Chrétien said, 'Get on to that right away.' But we were too slow."

2: ENLIST THE HOLY TRINITY

Since 1994, Campbell has tackled problems in terms of three letters: OST. O(bjective) is what you want to achieve, (S)trategy is the defining idea behind how you'll achieve it, and T(actics) are the literal things you will do. For most crises, the O is "survive"; S and T will depend on the crisis. The crucial task is to identify them, then rapidly centralize everybody involved to ensure all activity is planned and serves that OST. When drawing up tactics, one misconception is that it's best to make all information public immediately.

3: THE MESSAGE IS KING

You need to constantly narrate your strategy. During the Milošević crisis, for instance, "our message became: 'his troops out, our troops in, refugees go home.'" Good messages are not formulaic, defensive or repeated verbatim like a slogan (instead, mix up the wording yet retain the core idea). You also need to give the crisis a human face — but pick the best person. "So often with corporate crises they put up a guy who is brilliant at his day job, but like a frightened rabbit in front of a camera. The public don't care if the screen says 'chairman' or 'finance director.'" Finally, rebut false perceptions.

4: KNOW WHEN TO ADAPT

"If a problem persists that people can pick away at, you need to move into a different mode," says Campbell. "But the best adaptation comes when people don't necessarily notice." Take the royal family — in the mid-Nineties, British republicanism was growing. "They've seen that off by adapting very subtly. Look at the Queen. She has a Facebook page but the pictures on it are of her riding a horse. Letting tourists into Buckingham Palace and paying tax — these were also big steps."

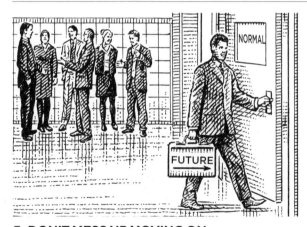

5: DON'T MESS UP MOVING ON

Even when it all seems hopeless, remember: the crisis will eventually be over. That's why somebody needs to be thinking about what you will do once things have returned to normal. "With all the strategies I was involved in, there was such a relief when they ended that you just take your eye off the ball for a bit." If you've had an oil spill, say, you might become a more meaningful champion of environmental policy. And sometimes you need a change of personnel to signal your fresh start. "Perhaps you put in a new boss."

8:

THE UNEXPECTED

Murphy's Law puts it simply: anything that can go wrong will go wrong. Keep that in mind when you read the guides in this chapter, which range from surviving a kidnapping to landing a plane with engine failure. We wanted to address even the most outlandish scenarios with real authority, so in this chapter you'll encounter people with some unusual backgrounds. There's a former member of SEAL Team Six, for example, and a man who has lived through a full-scale societal breakdown. If the worst happens, you'll have the very best shot at making it through...

SURVIVE A KIDNAPPING

>> A volley of gunfire told Andy McNab that he had been discovered. It was January 1991, during the thick of the Gulf War, and a few days earlier his SAS patrol had gone behind Iraqi lines. Soon after, the group had been compromised and started making its way toward Syria, trying to evade enemy forces. Now, he was being dragged from a drainage ditch where he had been hiding, and bundled into a Land Cruiser.

As described in his book *Bravo Two Zero* (1993), a bestseller that would kick-start his post-SAS career as an author, he would be held — interrogated, beaten and tortured — for six long weeks. In the unlikely event you ever find yourself taken captive, this is his advice on how to get through it...

1: BECOME THE GRAY MAN

Let's backtrack. The most important thing is not to get kidnapped in the first place, so don't present yourself as a person of value. "You've got a lot of rich guys in Moscow who drive ten-year-old Skodas," notes McNab. Give a false name whenever you book a cab to pick you up from an airport.

"At a lot of airports around the planet, you've got guys there with mobiles and laptops who'll look up the customer names on the waiting drivers' signs. If it's a high-value executive, well straight away that's a fantastic target."

2: CREATE DISTANCE

If somebody tries to kidnap you, time is of the essence. That means you should plan escape routes for any high-risk location. The crucial thing is to create distance between yourself and the problem: run to a safe place or jump from a window. If that's not possible, you should comply. "But every opportunity there is, you need to try to escape, no matter what — push and run." What if they're armed? "If they've got pistols, they've got to be really good shots to take you down at 5 meters [or 16ft] as a moving target."

3: FORGE A RELATIONSHIP

In captivity, you need to stay healthy. Avoid beatings by complying with demands and sympathizing with opinions. Your other priority is to make them see you as a human being. Tell them your name, and talk about your family (a well-prepared kidnapper will already know about your relatives so you're unlikely to put them at extra risk). Also, start smoking. "It's the universal bond. It gives you a mutual need with the captor. You get physical contact with their hands, because they're not going to let you use the lighter yourself. And also you get eye-to-eye contact when you're saying thank you."

4: DON'T LOSE YOUR MIND

While always looking to escape, accept your situation. "The only thing they haven't got control of is your mind, so get a grip." If they tell you that nobody wants to pay your ransom, don't believe it — it means nothing until it happens. As for staying sane in solitary confinement, McNab recalls an American pilot held in isolation for six years in Vietnam. "He built a house brick by brick in his head, working on it every day. Then he did the gardens. Once that was done, he said, 'Right, the house needs repainting...'"

5: PLAY THE ENDGAME

Relationship with your guards deteriorating? Being moved more frequently? Things are going wrong for your captors. If you suspect that they are about to kill you, you may as well fight — use your slop bucket, perhaps, or simply push your guard and run for it. "If the door in the corridor is locked, well, you're going to get shot — but you don't know..." On the other hand, rescue might be imminent. If special forces come in, discard any weapons, hit the ground — and don't grab the soldiers out of relief. "If you do that, they're all trained to drop [strike] you: you'll go down."

ESCAPE FROM A SINKING CAR

» If your car is going underwater, you have about a minute to get out alive. That's why Jon Ehm and Steffan Uzzell from Survival Systems USA recommend not calling the emergency services but immediately getting to work on the following technique. Their Connecticut-based company, founded in 1999, specializes in escaping from aircraft and vehicles underwater, and has trained special operations personnel, National Guard units and officers from federal law enforcement agencies. Most car submersions occur, says Ehm, when drivers get caught in a flood. "If people drown in a car, it's typically because they've driven into a situation deliberately: 'Oh there's water over the road, I'm just going to go ahead and risk it.'" Some situations, however, are less avoidable. Here's how to escape...

1: BRACE, BRACE, BRACE

If you are falling from a height — perhaps you have driven off a bridge or the side of a dock — prepare for impact. Keep your hands away from the airbag, gripping the steering wheel at the ten and two positions with your thumbs resting on the edge.

"You don't want to have your thumbs wrapped around the steering wheel as you could injure them," says Uzzell.

2: THE WINDOW OF OPPORTUNITY

Get your seatbelt off. The doors will be held shut by the water pressure, so rush to lower a window — this will be possible for approximately the first 30 seconds, while the car is still floating. Electric mechanisms should work up until that point, "Pretty much all manufacturers have a policy in place that the windows of their vehicles can be rolled down when the car is in water. Once the water reaches the edge of the windows, though, the pressure won't let them come down any more," says Uzzell.

3: ATTACK MODE ON

Window won't open? You will have to smash the glass. Take any sharp object or, failing that, your elbow, and attack the edge of the pane. Doing this underwater will cause a torrent of water and glass to rush in, so watch out. If the side windows are laminated safety glass, however, they will be difficult to break. In this instance, head to the back window. "The back window is probably not laminated, though you should plan ahead for your specific car," says Ehm. The back of the car is also where the final air pocket is going to be as the engine is the heaviest part of the vehicle and will sink first.

4: THE LAST RESORT

In the worst-case scenario, if you can't break any of the windows, wait until the car has completely filled with water. This will equalize the internal and external pressure and allow you to open the door. It will feel heavier than normal. "Try to remain as calm as possible, and relax as much as you can," says Ehm. That will help your breath last longer. You could easily drown in the process, so leaving earlier via the window is always preferable, not least because the door could be jammed.

5: THE GREAT ESCAPE

Once you have an exit point, pull yourself out and push away from the car frame. Swim toward the light — that's the surface. "If there's no light, put a hand over your mouth and blow some air out," says Uzzell. "You should feel the direction the bubbles are going, and orient yourself in that direction." Once you have emerged, if any part of the car is above the water, climb on top of it, wait for rescue and count your blessings.

SAVE YOURSELF FROM CHOKING

>> Dr. Nicholas Hopkinson puts it straightforwardly: "If you're in a situation where some food has gone down the wrong way, and you can't breathe and can't talk — if that isn't fixed, you're going to die." A respiratory specialist at London's Royal Brompton hospital, Hopkinson has co-authored research on the effectiveness of different techniques for treating blockages. As part of the project, he learned that two major risk times are at Sunday lunch ("Makes sense") and 7pm on a Wednesday night ("Who knows why that is?"). If you fall victim while alone, here's the optimum response...

1: RESPOND FAST

Try to hack up the blockage. Go outside to get help if you're somewhere populated.

2: DASH TO A CHAIR

No help available? Lean over a chair and position its back just under your ribcage.

3: APPLY PRESSURE

Use your arms to pull the chair into your upper abdomen with increasing force.

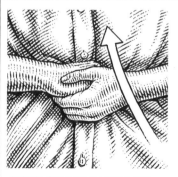

4: NO CHAIR IN SIGHT?

Bunch your fists above your navel and self-administer the Heimlich maneuver.

EVADE PURSUERS USING PARKOUR

>> When most people walk down the street they see confinements: staircases, rails, barriers — the lanes in which society tells us it is acceptable to travel. "When you've got a 'freerunner's eye,'" says Sam Parham, "you see all those things as opportunities — the whole world opens up and nowhere is off limits." Parham is a champion practitioner of parkour — the art of getting rapidly from A to B with athletics — and its flashier cousin, freerunning. Having won international competitions and bagged a world record (for the furthest double vault), the World Freerunning Parkour Federation athlete is fast racking up stuntman credits including *Game of Thrones* (2011–), *Star Wars: The Force Awakens* (2015) and *The Edge of Tomorrow* (2014). If you ever have to flee an assailant, his moves will give you an edge...

1: THE WALL RUN

Sprint at the wall and plant the ball of your foot at the optimum height to transfer horizontal energy into vertical. Parham is 1.7m (5½ft) tall, and he finds 75cm (2½ft) from the ground is about right. Kick once, explosively, to launch upward. Use your hands, palms flat against the wall, to guide you. Reach up to the top ledge with both hands — or one hand if you need extra reach — and use your momentum to kick upward from the wall again, first with one foot and then the other. Push yourself up on your arms and climb over.

2: THE ROLL LANDING

If you jump off an obstacle higher than head height, you need to dissipate the energy or risk getting injured. Land on the balls of your feet with your momentum going forward, and immediately bend your knees. Let your hands meet the floor, tuck in your chin and roll forward. "As you're landing on a hard surface, you don't want to roll directly over your head and spine," says Parham. Instead, roll diagonally over your shoulder and down to the opposite side of your lower back. Use your momentum to keep running.

3: THE CAT LEAP

If a jump is too far or too high to land on your feet, you could try a cat leap to grab the edge of the wall. From stationary, jump from the balls of your feet, throwing your arms fully forward. Focus on where you are going to land your hands. Midair, bring your feet in front of you to absorb the impact — they need to meet the wall either just before or at the same time as your hands. As you land, bend your knees. Note: you can also do a running jump, but this will result in a heavier landing.

4: THE SPEED VAULT

"The speed vault is known to be one of the most efficient routes over a wall, a rail — whatever it might be." Take off with one foot, about a meter (yard) from the obstacle, and drive the other foot up and over. Unlike traditional hurdling, however, you tilt your body to the side so you don't have to jump so high. As you fly forward, perform a scissor-kick to put your trailing leg out in front. Finally, put your hand on the obstacle to push your body upright again, before landing on your front foot and running on.

5: THE PRECISION JUMP

This is for when you need to "stick" a dangerous landing, so that you don't topple backward or get carried forward. From stationary, put your toes over the edge of the ledge on which you're standing and jump, driving your arms forward. Now, bring your legs forward so the balls of your feet meet the target slightly ahead of your body, and bend your knees prior to landing. Bend them further on impact to absorb the shock. But the most important part? Practice. "Sometimes I go out and just do 100 precision jumps, and that's my training for the day."

FEND OFF A DOG ATTACK

>> Clint Emerson knows how to handle himself. During his two decades in the US Navy, he conducted special operations internationally. His first attachment was to SEAL Team 3, a group instrumental in the 2003 invasion of Iraq. "I led the platoon that took down gas and oil platforms out in the Persian Gulf," says Emerson, author of the bestselling *100 Deadly Skills* (2015). When he returned to the US, he entered "more of a covert, clandestine world." He was later assigned to SEAL Team 6, the group that took out Osama Bin Laden. So neutralizing a dog attack? Child's play...

1: ASSESS THE THREAT

Look at the dog's body language. Warning signs: static tail, head held directly in line with the body, growling, baring teeth and walking toward you. If you see those behaviors, prepare to respond fast. "Dogs tend not to just hang out and wait."

2: TRY TO DEFUSE THE SITUATION

While you shouldn't run away or turn your back, try slowly backing away. Not working? Make yourself look big — spread your legs and wave your hands in the air — and shout. See if you can gain a height advantage by climbing on to an obstacle such as a car.

3: IF AN ATTACK IS INEVITABLE...

Take off your shirt or jacket and wrap it around your arm. Offer the dog this limb – but try to get it to bite the top of your arm, preferably near the elbow, as it's less likely to cause a major injury. "If you go further down your forearm, your arteries and veins are far shallower."

4: DEFEAT THE DOG

Don't rip your arm away or this will cause you injury. Instead, fall on the dog (if this isn't possible, grip the back of its head). Next, push your arm hard into its mouth — the dog will find this extremely uncomfortable. You can also strike the eyes, the muzzle or behind its front legs, which is a sensitive area.

5: TREAT YOUR WOUNDS

If you've caused enough pain, the dog will let you go and then you can create distance. You may well be bleeding. First, try elevation and direct pressure to stem the flow. If that doesn't work, tie a tourniquet above the wound. Seek medical attention as soon as possible.

SURVIVE A TSUNAMI

>> If you hear that a tsunami is on its way, disabuse yourself of the notion that it could be interesting to watch the water roll in. "Sometimes people think it's a bit of fun," says Jagan Chapagain, an Under Secretary General at the International Federation of Red Cross and Red Crescent Societies (IFRC). "It happens so rarely that the consequences are just not in people's heads." Caused by offshore earthquakes, volcanic activity or underwater landslides, a tsunami wave can measure hundreds of feet high and carry enormous force. "I was in Japan immediately after the tsunami [in 2011]. It brought utmost devastation to every single thing that came in its way. Human beings, cars, buildings, trees, power lines — absolute devastation." The Red Cross mobilizes after these disasters. However, a great deal of its work is on preparedness...

1: IF YOU HEAR A TSUNAMI WARNING, IT'S TIME TO GO

An earthquake may be the first sign that a tsunami's coming. "When that happens, listen to your community radio, government radio — keep your ears open — and use online systems." If a "tsunami watch" is issued, that means a tsunami is possible. You need to get at least 100m (330ft) above sea level or 3km (2 miles) inland. "That's the time to prepare your family, your pets, and evacuate." If a "tsunami warning" comes through, that means a wave has been generated. "You have very little time. Grab whatever you can and run." If you can see the wave, you're too close.

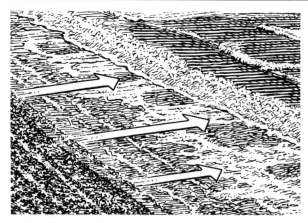

2: WATCH OUT FOR NATURAL SIGNS

Before a tsunami, you may see the ocean retreating from the shore dramatically. "Sometimes hundreds of meters could be dried out. The bigger the length, the bigger the danger sign. The 'good' thing is that, if that happens, it takes quite some time for the wave to come to the shore — sometimes a couple of hours." Also, watch out for animals behaving unusually. "When we're talking to the local communities, they say that they see that happen every single time."

3: IF YOU CAN'T FLEE, TRY TO GAIN HEIGHT

Higher ground is ideal because even sturdy structures can be demolished by a tsunami wave. If your only option is to run up a building, however, look for something made of concrete, ideally built by the authorities. "Generally in the developed world, where the building codes are strong, if you look at the hospitals, police stations and schools, the quality of construction is good. Though be aware that in many countries the building codes are not followed." As a last resort, if there are no buildings nearby, scale a strong-looking tree and hope for the best.

4: IN THE WATER? HOLD ON TIGHT

If you're caught up in the floodwater, you're in trouble. "The one piece of advice is to try to hold on to something." It may be tempting to climb on top of a car but actually this isn't advisable: the problem with metal structures is that they can get damaged relatively easily. Chapagain notes that people have survived tsunamis in the past by holding on to trees until they were rescued. Don't try to swim your way to safety – you have zero chance of success.

5: DON'T LET YOUR GUARD DOWN PREMATURELY

It's a common misconception that a tsunami is simply one giant wave. In reality, it's likely to be a sequence of waves, arriving as quickly as a few minutes after the first and often with greater magnitude. "But sometimes the wave can come after 10, 12 hours. Wait until the authorities say it's safe to go back."

That means, even if you're up a building, it's advisable to wait there until you have the all clear. When you venture out, keep away from downed power lines and watch out for structures, such as bridges, that could potentially collapse.

FIND OUT IF YOU'RE BEING FOLLOWED

» Are you being watched? Intelligence professionals routinely use anti-surveillance drills to answer that very question — and in an age where corporate espionage is big business, these can be just as useful to the layperson. "You might be an executive in confidential talks with another company, perhaps, or a journalist meeting a source," says Peter Jenkins. "It could be wise to carry out some drills to make sure you're not being followed." A former Royal Marine Commando specializing in intelligence and counterterrorism, Jenkins now runs the surveillance tuition company ISS Training, which he set up in 1990. Its clients hail from 17 countries worldwide and include diplomatic security teams, national intelligence services, federal police forces and close protection officers. Here's a mini masterclass…

1: THE RULE OF THREE

The following drills are designed to help you identify surveillance teams. But what exactly are you looking for? The main thing is spotting the same person in three different places. The other red flag is unnatural behavior such as someone gazing into space, talking into their collar or copying your actions. If you are suspicious of someone, note their shoes. "On the move, surveillance teams can easily change their coats, or a female operative could take off her long skirt and have jeans underneath. But the shoes are probably going to stay the same."

»

2: TAKE A WALK

On foot, head away from the bustle. Look behind you frequently to make checks, but do be covert about it. Methods include doing so while holding a door for somebody, or pretending to push the button at a pedestrian crossing and glancing up and down the road, ostensibly at the traffic. You can also flush out surveillance by walking through "choke points," such as narrow walkways, or heading into a shopping mall. For the latter, get out of sight and watch the entranceway for suspicious behavior.

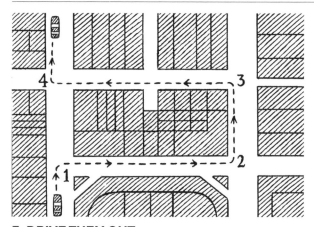

3: DRIVE THEM OUT

When you're in a car, a classic drill is driving "three sides of a square." Keep an eye on your mirrors as you take the detour shown. If a car stays on your tail throughout, when it could simply have carried on straight down the road, that's highly suspect. You may not want to alert the surveillance team that you're on to them. Create a reason for your strange route. "Stop after one of the turns, go to a newsagents, get back in the car and drive off. You have done the same thing but now you've made it more covert."

4: RIG YOUR PROPERTY

Those who believe they are under surveillance could buy a motion camera to see if anyone enters their house — but when time is tight, there are some old-fashioned techniques that can also be useful. You could put a small piece of tape where the top of a door meets the doorframe. Should anyone open the door, the tape will come unstuck but the intruder will be none the wiser. "Or you could brush a piece of carpet one way, and then you'll see indents in the carpet if someone walks on it."

5: SO, YOU'RE UNDER SURVEILLANCE — NOW WHAT?

Keep a clear head. If you feel endangered, notify the police. You may, however, prefer to call out the surveillance team. Confronting them is an option, but it might be smarter to ask them for the time or directions. "That will really spook them." Either way, supposing that you do have a secret to protect, you'll need to be careful from now on. "Certainly what I wouldn't do, if I were on the move when I detected surveillance, is carry on to where I'm going. Their aim might simply be to find out where I end up."

LAND A PLANE WITH ENGINE FAILURE

>> You're traveling in a light aircraft. Yes, an engine failure is unlikely. Yes, it's even more unlikely that the pilot will be incapacitated and it will be up to you to land the plane. But Finagle's Law dictates that anything that can go wrong, will – at the worst possible moment. So wouldn't you rather know what you're doing if it did? We asked Captain Rob Sedgwick for a primer. Sedgwick spent his career flying commercial airliners, including the Boeing 737, 747 and 777. Now, he works at the training company Virtual Aviation. All pilots, he says, have to prepare for scenarios such as engine failures. "When you join an airline, there's quite an involved simulator course, which basically throws every conceivable 'non-normal' situation or fault at you." Here's what you would do if it happened for real...

1: ASK FOR HELP

"Initially, you'll try to restart the engine," says Sedgwick. Simply turn the key (8 in the next image). If that doesn't work or the pilot is still out of action, you need to ask for help. Put on the headset, press the talk button (7) and say, "Mayday, mayday, mayday," followed by the plane's unique registration. This is usually on a placard on the instrument panel. No response? Try the standard emergency frequency, 121.5, on the radio (6). Next, look for the transponder (5), a box labelled, usually, XPDR or TP, displaying four digits. Dial 7700 to put others on alert.

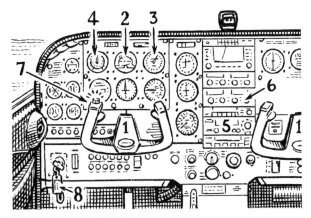

2: TAKE CONTROL

If you can get through to someone on the radio, they will be able to talk you through landing the plane. Whether you have assistance or not, however, the procedure is the same. First, take hold of the control yoke (1). Pushing it forward makes the nose dip, pulling it back pulls the nose up, left turns the plane left, and vice-versa. Also, locate your key instruments: the artificial horizon (2), which will show you if you're level; altimeter (3), which measures height; and airspeed indicator (4).

3: GIVE YOURSELF TIME

Aircrafts with engines will glide, but they will descend faster than a purpose-built glider so, if you have enough airspeed (perhaps the plane was in a dive), see if you can climb. "The higher you are, the more time you have to sort out whatever your problem is." As you do so, beware of stalling — this is when the plane's angle is such that the speed slows to the extent that you fail to generate lift. If this happens, it will cause the plane to shudder and a warning tone to sound. To fix it, push the nose down until the warning stops.

4: LOOK FOR A PLACE TO LAND

If you're near a runway, head to it. "Any runway is better than no runway, because it will have emergency services and crash facilities." If there's no airport nearby, look for large roads, but be mindful of cars. "The problem is that major roads have got bridges across them, but it's better than landing in a field. If you're looking for fields, you're looking for a smooth field, not a ploughed field. Golf courses are quite good places, apparently."

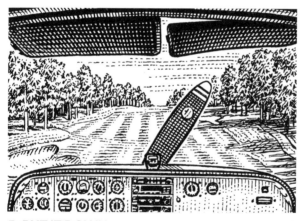

5: PUT IT DOWN

Use your intuition to control the descent. If you can fit your fist in the gap between the plane's nose and the horizon, that's about right. "It should be a flatter landing than if you had power available. The idea would be to get somewhere over the landing area, let the airplane fly as low as you think you can, and just flare at the last minute." To flare, pull back gently on the stick before you hit the ground. To brake, push the top of the rudder pedals with your toes. If you made it one piece, thank your guardian angels.

MAKE IT THROUGH THE APOCALYPSE

>> "As soon as things fall apart, people show their real faces," says Selco Begovic. "You would be amazed at how many bad people are around you." Begovic knows of what he speaks. During the Bosnian conflict in the early Nineties he survived in a city under siege for a year, cut off from food, electricity and the rule of law. Now, he runs SHTF School (that stands for "Sh*t Hits The Fan") to share what he learned with survivalists who not only wish to prepare for a catastrophic scenario, but also want the certainty that what they're being taught is useful. "Survival is a huge industry but it's full of lies," he says. His experience means that this advice on what to do if society breaks down is the real deal...

1: PACK A "BUG OUT" BAG

This is a bag that contains the essentials you will need when leaving town. Have all the possible equipment laid out on shelves, so you can quickly select the bare minimum for the situation. Think about shelter, hygiene, food, fire, water, tools, clothes and footwear. Also have three bag options: a small backpack, a suitcase and a military-style backpack. Judge what to take depending on how long you'll be bugging out for, and what is least likely to attract attention. If the rule of law has totally collapsed, a suitcase, for instance, may entice people to rob you.

2: FOLLOW YOUR PLAN

You should have identified a safe haven, where you will go in the event of a disaster, and friends that will go there with you. "Many people imagine that a safe haven is a small cabin in the wilderness. But it is impossible for ordinary city people to live and survive in the wilderness." Instead, arrange a place of refuge in a small village community where there are people you know. Prepare various routes and means for getting there, avoiding high-risk areas, such as bridges, inner cities and gas stations.

3: THINK BEYOND MONEY

In the short term, money will be useful. In the long term, less so. Some survivalists obsess over buying gold bars. "Actually, if you want to buy something to trade later, I suggest you buy 100 or 1,000 cheap lighters rather than 100g [3½oz] of gold." If you do want to store some gold for bigger purchases, keep it in small quantities — 30 gold rings, say. A single ring is a more practical unit of exchange, and you can take it off your finger and hand it over like it's your only one, rather than part of a stash. That's much safer.

4: HAVE A FOOD STRATEGY

If you think you will simply start producing your own food, check yourself. "People from urban areas don't realize how much effort they'll need to put in." That's why you must have a stash of six months' to a year's worth of food in your safe haven. You will need to have established connections with those nearby who can farm, and start building a small farm yourself. Focus on chickens and rabbits — they take little time and effort to rear — as well as potatoes and beans because they will grow almost anywhere.

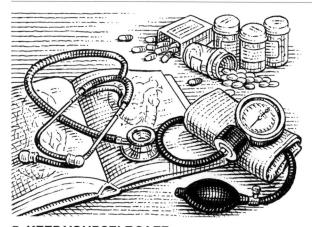

5: KEEP YOURSELF SAFE

If guns are legal in your country, Begovic advises tooling up. Choose weapons that are commonly available so you can easily get hold of extra ammo. If guns are illegal, you should still learn how to handle one, just in case. Perhaps the biggest threat to your safety, however, is your health. Make sure you have diarrhea medicine — stomach bugs will be rife — and those with a medical condition should learn as much as possible about it and stockpile relevant treatment. "You need to understand that there will be no medical system, so you need to be your own physician."

INDEX

THANKS

» First and foremost, I would like to thank all those who generously let me interview them for this book. It could not have happened without them and I hope they feel I did justice to their insights. It would also not be half the book it is without Dave Hopkins' meticulous illustrations. It has been a pleasure to work with him.

I owe an enormous debt to *GQ*'s Editor, Dylan Jones, for taking me on all those years ago, and for his support and encouragement. I am extremely grateful to Bill Prince, both for his counsel and for helping create the original column that inspired this book, and to the powerhouse that is Harriet Wilson for making it all happen. Thanks also to Paul Henderson, Jonathan Heaf, Stuart McGurk, Paul Solomons, Oliver Jamieson, Eleanor Halls, George Chesterton, Mark Russell, Agnes Bataclan and everyone at *GQ*.

My huge appreciation to Octopus Publishing: Joe Cottington for commissioning the project; Sybella Stephens for her editorial prowess; Jonathan Christie for his creative direction. Thanks to my agent Ben Clark, who also secured two of the interviewees, and the whole team at LAW.

Above all, my love and gratitude to my family, especially Emily, who helped in a thousand ways – even while we were planning our wedding.